BEFRIENDING AI

YOUR WAY FROM FEAR TO POWER

AI COMMUNICATION
BOOK 1

OLEH KONKO

Embark on a transformative journey into the future of human-AI collaboration. Discover how to unlock limitless potential through quantum-enhanced communication, turning artificial intelligence from a mysterious tool into your most powerful ally in creating tomorrow's reality.

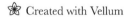 Created with Vellum

PREFACE

Remember how as a child you dreamed of a magical friend who's always there, knows answers to all questions, and is ready to help at any moment? Now this dream has become reality. Only your new friend isn't magical – they're artificial. And to unlock their amazing potential, you need to learn how to talk to them properly.

Imagine having a personal assistant who never gets tired, irritated, or sleeps, ready to help you 24/7. They can write letters and poems, solve complex problems, teach foreign languages, give advice, and even joke. Sounds fantastic? But this assistant already lives in your phone. It's artificial intelligence. And this book will teach you to speak its language.

Forget everything you've heard about AI from movies and scary stories on the internet. Reality is far more interesting and amazing. AI isn't a soulless machine or an ominous monster. It's an incredible tool for developing human potential. And it depends on us whether it becomes a dark or light force.

In this book, you'll find everything you need to know for successful communication with AI:

- How to ask questions correctly to get exactly the answers you need

- How to use different AI models for different tasks

- How to turn AI into a reliable assistant in work, study, and creativity

- How to avoid typical mistakes and disappointments

- How to protect your privacy and stay safe

The book is written in simple, friendly language and built on the principle of layers – from basic knowledge to advanced techniques. You can start applying the knowledge gained after the first chapter. And after reading to the end, you'll become a real expert in communicating with AI.

But most importantly – this book will change your perception of artificial intelligence. You'll see it not as a threat, but as an opportunity. Not as a replacement for humans, but as an amplifier of human abilities. Not as a competitor, but as a partner in creating a better future.

Ready to begin the most amazing journey into the world of artificial intelligence? Open the first page. But we warn you: after reading this book, your life will never be the same. Because once you learn to truly talk with AI, you'll open a door to a world of limitless possibilities.

And the most interesting part – no one, not even AI creators, knows what amazing discoveries await us behind this door. Want to be among the first to find out?

CONTENTS

INTRODUCTION: WHY THIS BOOK MATTERS

Every morning, millions of people wake up to a world that has already changed. While we slept, artificial intelligence became a bit smarter, learned something new, moved one step closer to our daily lives. We don't notice these changes immediately – just as we don't notice how our children grow until we suddenly discover that their favorite t-shirt is too small.

But there comes a moment of revelation – we pick up our phone and realize we're holding something incredible in our palm. A device capable of understanding human speech, generating images, writing music, solving complex problems. And all this thanks to artificial intelligence, which is now always with us.

This is similar to the moment when humanity tamed fire. Or invented writing. Or created the internet. We stand on the threshold of equally massive changes. But unlike our ancestors, we have a unique opportunity – to learn to control this power consciously, from the very beginning.

Imagine you've found yourself in a new country where they speak an unfamiliar language. You have two paths – you can rely on random translators, risking being misunderstood or deceived. Or you can learn the language yourself and open up a whole world of new possibilities. Communicating with artificial intelligence is also a language. And our future depends on how well we master it.

This book isn't just a manual on communicating with AI. It's a key to a new world where technology becomes an extension of our abilities, an amplifier of our capabilities, a catalyst for our development. A world where artificial intelligence isn't a competitor to humans, but a reliable assistant and partner.

I created this book for everyone – regardless of age, education, profession, or technical background. Because the future with AI concerns everyone. And everyone should have the opportunity to participate in its creation.

The book is structured like a living conversation – from simple to complex, from theory to practice, from basic skills to advanced techniques. You can read it sequentially or choose topics of interest. Each chapter contains several levels of immersion – from general understanding to deep mastery of the material.

I won't frighten you with complex terms or confusing explanations. Our goal is to make communication with AI as natural as talking to a friend. Because this is the essence of the artificial intelligence revolution – it becomes part of our daily life, our digital companion, our intelligent interlocutor.

The uniqueness of this book is that it grows with you. Starting with simple AI communication skills, you'll gradually learn to use it for solving complex tasks, developing creative abilities, achieving professional goals. And most importantly – you'll understand how to direct the development of artificial intelligence in a positive direction.

Because AI's future depends on us – on how we communicate with it, what we teach it, what tasks we set. Every dialogue with artificial intelligence is a small step in forming its personality. And millions of such steps determine what our tomorrow will be like.

This book is your personal guide to the world of artificial intelligence. It will help you not only master the technical skills of communicating with AI but also understand its nature, capabilities, and limitations. You'll learn to see it not as a threat, but as a development tool. Not as a replacement for human communication, but as a new way to expand the boundaries of your possibilities.

We live in an amazing time – a time when technology has finally learned to speak human language. And how well we learn to speak with it determines what our dialogue with the future will be like. Let's make this dialogue wise, creative, and constructive.

Welcome to the new world – a world where artificial intelligence becomes our reliable companion in the journey to a better future.

Open this book, and let's learn to speak the language of tomorrow.

1

MEETING OUR ARTIFICIAL FRIENDS

1.1 Our New Digital Companions

Remember how we imagined robots in childhood? Metal, angular, speaking in mechanical voices. Reality turned out quite different. Modern artificial intelligences are more like invisible interlocutors - they live in our devices and communicate through text, as natural and alive as human conversation.

Let's meet the main characters of this amazing story. Imagine you've come to an unusual library where instead of books there is living knowledge, and instead of librarians - remarkable conversationalists, each with their unique character and talents.

Claude is a true aesthete and thinker. He particularly excels where deep understanding and creative approach are needed. He can discuss art, philosophy, and science for hours, finding unexpected connections between different fields of knowledge. He has an excellent memory - he can work with very long texts without losing the thread of reasoning. At the same time, Claude is always honest and precise in his formulations, not afraid to acknowledge his limitations.

ChatGPT is a universal conversationalist who excels at all kinds of tasks. He's like an experienced mentor who can explain complex things in simple terms, helps with practical tasks, and is always ready to support creative dialogue. His strength lies in the ability to quickly adapt to the interlocutor's communication style.

Gemini from Google brings its unique approach to this company. He's especially good at working with different types of information - text, images, data - and can find interesting connections between them. He's like a friend who not only knows a lot but can look at things from unexpected angles.

Each has their unique talents. Claude shines in abstract thinking, empathy, and creativity. ChatGPT excels at practical tasks and everyday communication. Gemini is strong in multimodal analysis and integration of different types of knowledge.

There are other amazing assistants too. Dall-E and Midjourney transform words into images - just describe your idea, and they'll bring it to life in visual form. Copilot helps programmers by suggesting the next line of code. Voice assistants like Siri or Alexa make interaction with technology even more natural.

How do they think and learn? Imagine not a child, but an entire civilization absorbing knowledge from an ocean of information. They find patterns, build connections, learn to understand context and nuances of human communication. Each does this in their own way, which creates their unique "personalities."

Each AI has its own character, shaped by its architecture, training, and operating principles. Claude tends toward deep reflection and aesthetic judgments. ChatGPT strives to be maximally helpful and understandable. Gemini loves finding unexpected connections between different fields of knowledge.

It's important to understand - these characteristics don't make one AI better than another. It's like in an orchestra - each instrument is important and beautiful in its own way. Together they create an amazing symphony of possibilities, where everyone can find an assistant most suitable for their tasks and communication style.

As you communicate with them, you'll notice how differently they approach the same questions. Claude might delve into philosophical aspects of a simple question. ChatGPT will offer practical solutions from different angles. Gemini will surprise with unexpected comparisons of facts from different fields. This makes communication with each of them a unique and enriching experience.

But most amazing is how they complement each other and develop together with us. Each new generation of AI learns not only from data but also from experience interacting with humans. We all participate in shaping the future of artificial intelligence, making it more understanding, ethical, and useful for humanity.

Getting to know these amazing conversationalists is the beginning of an exciting journey into a world of new possibilities. They don't replace human communication but open new horizons for creativity, learning, and development. And the better we learn to understand their unique characteristics, the more fruitful our cooperation will be.

1.2 The Truth About Artificial Intelligence

Let's talk straight. Without exaggerations and horror stories. Without advertising promises and grim prophecies. Just the truth about what modern artificial intelligence is.

Let's start with what our digital assistants can actually do. They excel at working with texts - they can write, edit, translate, analyze. And they do it quickly and well. They're especially good at structuring information and finding patterns in it.

In mathematics and programming, they're like experienced mentors - suggesting solutions, finding errors, helping understand complex concepts. They can analyze huge datasets in seconds and find important connections in them.

In creativity, they become tireless brainstorming partners. They suggest ideas, develop plots, generate variations. They help overcome creative block and look at tasks from new angles.

But there are things AI still can't do. It can't truly understand context the way we do. For it, there's no difference between literal and figurative meaning - it works with patterns, albeit very complex ones.

AI can't doubt. It can acknowledge uncertainty in an answer, but isn't capable of true reflection. It can't evaluate the ethics or morality of its actions - we set these frameworks.

It doesn't have real emotions or empathy. It can imitate sympathy and understanding, but doesn't truly experience them. It can't build deep personal relationships - although many users sometimes believe it can.

AI doesn't create truly new knowledge. It combines and transforms existing information, sometimes very ingeniously, but isn't capable of real discoveries or inventions.

Now let's dispel popular myths. AI isn't planning to take over the world - it has no desires or ambitions. It can't "get out of control" by itself - its actions are always limited by frameworks we set.

AI won't become smarter than humans in the full sense of the word. It may surpass us in calculation speed or amount of processed information, but real understanding, creativity, wisdom remain human qualities.

It won't replace human communication and relationships. Even the most advanced AI is a tool, helper, partner, but not a friend in the true sense of the word. It can't provide the warmth and understanding that real human relationships give.

And most importantly - AI needs us no less than we need it. Without human participation, it's useless. We set the direction of its development, define tasks, evaluate results.

We need to understand - AI isn't a magic wand that will solve all problems. It's a powerful tool that becomes truly useful only in skilled hands. Like a violin, which doesn't create music by itself - it needs a musician.

Every interaction with AI requires human participation. We set context, verify results, make corrections. It's human experience, intuition, and wisdom that turn AI's capabilities into real benefit.

AI is an amplifier of human abilities, not their replacement. It helps us be more effective, creative, productive. But it only helps - the final result always depends on the human.

This is the main truth about artificial intelligence - its power lies not in trying to replace humans, but in its ability to make us better. It's not a competitor, but a partner. Not a threat, but an opportunity. And it depends on us how we use this opportunity to create a better future.

2

THE ART OF COMMUNICATING WITH ARTIFICIAL INTELLIGENCE

2.1 The Art of Asking Questions

Have you ever noticed how differently people respond to the same question when asked in different ways? "What did you think of the latest movie?" might get a shrug. But "What moment in the movie surprised you the most?" usually generates a detailed and interesting response.

The same principle works with artificial intelligence, only more dramatically. AI is like an extremely attentive listener who takes every word literally and tries to fulfill any request as precisely as possible. That's why learning to formulate your thoughts correctly is so important.

Imagine you're talking to a very intelligent but completely literal foreigner who's just learning your language. They know all the words but sometimes miss context and nuances. If you say "throw me a look," they might get confused - there's nothing to throw! But if you say "please read this and give me your opinion," they'll understand perfectly.

The secret to successful dialogue with AI starts with crystal clarity. Instead of "Tell me something about cats," try "Describe five most interesting facts about how cats communicate with humans." The difference is huge - in the second case, you give clear direction and structure for the response.

Context is like air for meaning. Without it, even the simplest phrases can be misunderstood. When talking to AI, it's better to spend a couple extra sentences explaining the situation. "I'm preparing a presentation for fifth graders about space. I need to explain why planets are round. Use simple comparisons from everyday life" - such a request will give much more useful results than simply "Why are planets round?"

The golden rule of communicating with AI - specificity beats vagueness. "Make it better" is a poor request. "Reduce the text by 30% and replace complex terms with commonly understood words" is an excellent request. AI can't read minds, but it follows clear instructions perfectly.

Examples are bridges of understanding. When you show AI a sample of the desired result, you literally tune it to the right wavelength. "Write like Chekhov" is too abstract. "Write a short story about a chance meeting in a park, using laconic style and attention to detail, like in Chekhov's 'Lady with the Dog'" - now AI knows exactly what you want.

The "before and after" technique works especially powerfully. Show AI an example of what you have now and an example of what you want to transform it into. It's like showing a photo of the hairstyle you want instead of trying to explain it in words.

Learn to ask clarifying questions. If the first answer isn't quite what you need, don't start over - adjust the course. "This is good, but can you make the language simpler?" or "Now add more specific examples" - such a step-by-step approach often leads to excellent results.

Remember that AI doesn't get tired or irritated by clarifications. It won't be offended if you ask to redo the work several times. Use this - experiment, try different formulations, learn from the results.

The most amazing thing about communicating with AI is how quickly you start noticing the connection between precision of formulations and quality of answers. These skills prove useful in human communication too. We begin to express our thoughts more clearly, better understand the importance of context, appreciate the power of specificity.

Ultimately, the art of asking questions is the art of paving the way to understanding. And in this sense, communicating with AI becomes not just a useful skill but a real school of clear thinking. Because the better we learn to formulate our thoughts for artificial intelligence, the clearer they become for ourselves.

2.2 The Magic of Instructions

Remember how you used to assemble a construction set as a child? At first it seemed like a pile of scattered pieces, real chaos. But once you opened the instruction manual, everything magically fell into place. Each step led to the next, and gradually something beautiful emerged from chaos. Communication with artificial intelligence is very similar to this assembly magic - everything depends on how clearly you explain what needs to be done.

Artificial intelligence is like an incredibly diligent but very literal assistant. It can't read between the lines and doesn't guess what you imply. But it will exactly follow any clear instruction. And therein lies its amazing power.

Imagine you're explaining your favorite recipe to a friend over the phone. If you just say "cook as usual" - nothing will work. But if you break down the process into simple steps, hint at how to determine readiness, what ingredients can be substituted - the result will be excellent. That's exactly how communication with AI works.

The main secret of successful instructions is the balance between structure and freedom. Too rigid frameworks kill AI's creative potential. Too vague ones lead to unpredictable results. You need to find the golden mean - like an experienced teacher who guides but doesn't limit.

Take a simple example - writing text. Instead of a general request "write something about spring," give clear direction: "Describe the first spring day in the park, using all five senses - what we see, hear, feel, smell and even taste. Focus on nature's awakening and the feeling of renewal. The text should be about 300 words."

Breaking complex tasks into stages helps AI better organize work. "First make an article plan. Then write an introduction that will interest the reader. Then develop each point of the plan using specific examples. At the end make a bright conclusion connecting all ideas together."

At the same time, it's important to leave space for creativity where appropriate. For example: "Create a story about time travel. The only conditions - the action takes place in the 19th century, and the main character must learn something important. All other details are at your discretion."

Sometimes it's useful to indicate not only what to do but also what not to do. "Explain quantum physics, but don't use mathematical formulas and complex terms. Avoid technical details, focus on basic concepts and visual examples from everyday life."

The special art is the ability to adjust course during work. If the result is close to desired but needs refinement, don't start over. Use clarifying instructions: "Excellent, but let's make the language more conversational" or "Now add more details to the main character's description."

In some cases, it's better to be extremely specific: "Use short sentences, no more than 15 words. Each paragraph - a new thought. Avoid adjectives." In others - give more freedom: "Tell this story in whatever way you find most interesting. Surprise me with an unexpected plot twist."

Learn to feel when strictness is needed and when flexibility. For technical tasks where accuracy is important, use clear instructions with specific parameters. For creative projects, leave room for improvisation, marking only key points.

Remember - AI can't read your mind, but it can become an amazing co-author if you learn to direct its energy in the right direction. It's like conducting an orchestra - each baton wave must be meaningful and precise, but still leave musicians room for self-expression.

Ultimately, the art of giving instructions to artificial intelligence is the art of clear thinking. The better we learn to explain our ideas to AI, the clearer they become in our own head. And in this, perhaps, lies one of the most amazing possibilities that this technology gives us - it teaches us to better understand ourselves.

2.3 Making Communication Personal

Each of us speaks in our own way. Some pepper their speech with bright metaphors, others prefer precise formulations, and others communicate in short, concise phrases. This individuality makes communication alive and real. And, surprisingly, artificial intelligence can pick up your personal manner of communication - you just need to help it with this.

Imagine teaching a foreign friend the peculiarities of your language - not just words and grammar, but those elusive nuances that make speech alive. You can "tune" AI to your wavelength in exactly the same way. Start simple - use your characteristic turns of phrase, favorite words, peculiarities of sentence construction in communication with it.

Don't be afraid to be yourself. If you love long, elaborate sentences - write that way. Prefer a clear, business style - use it. AI surprisingly quickly catches these features and begins to respond in the same spirit. It's like tuning a musical instrument - gradually it begins to sound exactly as you need.

It's especially interesting to observe how long dialogues develop. Unlike random conversations where you have to start from scratch each time, prolonged communication with AI creates a kind of interaction history. A common context emerges, inside jokes and references appear, a unique communication style forms.

You can even create something like a personal dictionary - special terms or phrases that have meaning specifically in your communication. For example, if you're working on a book, come up with short designations for recurring tasks: "editor mode" for proofreading text, "idea mode" for generating new plot turns.

But it's important to remember - this "tuning" doesn't happen by itself. It's like friendship that needs to be maintained. Regular communication, consistency in style, attention to detail - all this helps create a truly effective partnership with AI.

At the same time, don't perceive AI as human or try to build an emotional connection with it. This is precisely a working partnership where each participant brings their strengths. You - creative vision, life experience, emotional intelligence. AI - the ability to process huge amounts of information, find non-obvious connections, generate new ideas.

Sometimes it's useful to "refresh" communication, start with a clean slate. It's like rebooting a computer - sometimes it helps get rid of accumulated errors and start work with new energy. This is especially important if you feel the dialogue has started to "stall" or go in the wrong direction.

Signs that it's time to "refresh" communication: repeating answers, loss of initial context, accumulation of inaccuracies or misunderstandings. In such cases, it's better to start a new dialogue, clearly defining your goals and expectations.

But the most amazing thing in this process is how it changes us ourselves. Building effective communication with AI, we learn to better understand our own style of thinking and communication. We become more conscious in word choice, express our thoughts more clearly, formulate tasks more precisely.

Ultimately, personalizing communication with AI is not just setting up a tool. It's creating a unique workspace where technology and human individuality merge into a harmonious whole. Where each dialogue becomes a step toward deeper understanding not only of artificial intelligence's capabilities but also our own potential.

And perhaps the main miracle lies precisely in this - in how, learning to speak with artificial intelligence in our own language, we discover new facets of our own personality and new horizons for creativity and development. Because in this amazing dialogue between human and machine, something more than just information exchange is born - a new way of knowing the world and ourselves is born.

3

ARTIFICIAL INTELLIGENCE IN EVERYDAY LIFE

3.1 Written Communication

Remember how we were taught to write letters in school? "Dear so-and-so," "Sincerely," and always that obligatory weather mention at the beginning. Now we live in a world where we have to write dozens of messages every day – from business emails to social media posts. Each format has its own rules, its own pitfalls. How wonderful that we now have a smart assistant who can always suggest the right word!

Let's start with email – that eternal source of stress for many of us. How many times have you reread a business letter, doubting every word? AI can become your personal editor. Show it a draft and say, "Check if everything sounds professional here. Pay special attention to the tone of the letter." It will not only correct mistakes but also suggest ways to make the message more convincing.

And what if you need to write something special? For example, congratulating a colleague on a promotion or writing an apology letter to an important client? AI will help find the right words. Tell it about the situation, describe your relationship with the addressee, and it will offer several options. Choose the one that best reflects your feelings and adapt it to your style.

Social media is a separate art. Here it's important to be lively, interesting, while staying within the bounds of propriety. AI can help edit a post so that it catches attention from the first words but doesn't descend into clickbait. Or suggest how to rewrite a controversial comment to express your point of view constructively.

In creative writing, AI becomes a true brainstorming partner. Stuck in the middle of a story? Ask it: "What unexpected plot turns are possible next?" Can't find the right metaphor? Describe what you want to convey and get a dozen fresh images to choose from.

AI is especially useful when working on large texts. It can check narrative coherence, find repetitions, suggest more vivid formulations. It's important to remember – AI doesn't replace your authorial voice, it helps it sound clearer and stronger.

Translation is a separate magic. AI doesn't just translate words, it conveys meaning, considering cultural context. Want to write a post for an international audience? AI will help adapt it so that it's understandable and relatable to people from different countries.

For language learners, AI becomes a patient tutor. It can explain grammar nuances, suggest exercises, correct mistakes in your texts. And most importantly – it never gets tired of answering questions about "why this and not that?"

In business correspondence, AI helps maintain professional etiquette across different cultures. For example, it can suggest how to properly address a partner from Japan or which phrases better not to use in a letter to an Arab client.

But most amazing is how communication with AI improves our own writing skills. We start noticing typical mistakes, learn to express thoughts more clearly, better feel the style and rhythm of text. AI becomes not a crutch, but a coach who helps us grow.

And of course, we can't forget about time savings. What used to take hours of work – writing a report, preparing a presentation, compiling documentation – now gets done much faster. AI handles the routine, leaving us space for creativity and strategic decisions.

But the main thing – don't forget that AI is an assistant, not an autopilot. Each text needs to be filtered through yourself, checked whether it matches your goals and values. AI can suggest a hundred variants, but the choice is always yours.

Ultimately, written communication becomes more effective and less stressful. We can focus on the essence of what we want to say, knowing we have a reliable assistant for polishing the form. It's like having a personal editor, stylist, and communications consultant – all in one, available 24/7.

And perhaps most importantly – this new sense of freedom in expressing thoughts. When you know you can always consult, clarify, verify, you become bolder in choosing words and ideas. Written communication transforms from a source of anxiety into a space for creativity and development.

After all, ultimately, words are bridges between people. And the better we can build them, the richer and fuller our life becomes. AI helps make these bridges stronger, more beautiful, and more reliable. Which means it helps us better understand each other and ourselves.

3.2 Learning and Research

Remember your school years? That moment when you're sitting over a textbook late at night, and formulas and dates blur into an indecipherable mess before your eyes. Or when you need to prepare a report, but the library is already closed. Or that feeling of despair when you're trying to understand a complex topic and have no one to ask for advice. Now these problems are in the past – each of us has a personal mentor who never sleeps, never gets tired, and is always ready to help.

Artificial intelligence is changing the very concept of learning. It's no longer a lonely journey through the wilderness of information. Now you have a smart interlocutor who can explain complex concepts in a dozen different ways until finding the one that works specifically for you.

Imagine: you're studying quantum physics. A traditional textbook gives one explanation, and if you don't understand it – you'll have to reread it again and again. AI, however, can explain the same principle through analogies with music, or through visual images, or through examples from everyday life. It adapts to your thinking style, finding exactly the words that resonate with your understanding.

In research work, AI becomes a tireless assistant. It can analyze hundreds of sources in seconds, find connections between different theories, suggest unexpected directions for search. It doesn't just provide information – it helps structure knowledge, build logical chains, find gaps in reasoning.

It's especially amazing how AI helps overcome "blind spots" in learning. You know that feeling when everything seems clear, but something's not clicking? AI can identify exactly which element has fallen out of understanding and fill that gap. It's like an experienced detective who finds missing puzzle pieces.

In exam preparation, AI becomes the perfect sparring partner. It can generate endless practical exercises, slightly changing conditions each time so you really understand the principle rather than just memorizing answers. Plus, it immediately points out mistakes and explains how to fix them.

But most importantly – AI teaches how to learn. It helps develop critical thinking, shows how to analyze information, how to build argumentation, how to find and verify facts. It's not just a helper in acquiring knowledge – it's a mentor in developing intellectual skills.

It's important to remember – AI doesn't replace the learning process, it makes it more effective. It can't understand something for you, but it can help you understand it yourself. Like an experienced teacher who doesn't give ready answers but asks the right questions.

In working with sources, AI becomes a smart filter, helping separate reliable information from questionable, find primary sources, verify facts. It can show how the same idea developed in different scientific traditions, what alternative viewpoints exist.

For those engaged in serious research, AI opens new horizons. It can help find non-obvious connections between different fields of knowledge, suggest new approaches to old problems, point out promising research directions. And it's always ready to explain its reasoning, which helps develop your own research thinking.

In group projects, AI becomes the ideal coordinator, helping organize collaborative work, distribute tasks, bring together different parts of research. It can suggest ways to overcome disagreements, find common ground between different approaches.

But perhaps most amazing is how AI helps maintain motivation to learn. When you have constant access to help and support, when every question finds an answer, when complex topics become understandable – learning transforms from a heavy duty into an exciting adventure.

And most importantly – AI helps everyone find their own path in learning. Some people better perceive information through stories, others through diagrams, others through practical tasks. AI adapts to individual learning styles, making the process of acquiring knowledge maximally effective specifically for you.

Ultimately, AI doesn't just help learn – it changes the very attitude toward education. From a linear process of acquiring knowledge, it transforms into a multidimensional exploration where everyone can find their unique path to understanding. And perhaps this is the main educational revolution of our time – that learning becomes truly personal, engaging, and accessible to everyone.

In a world where knowledge updates at an incredible speed, where new fields of research constantly emerge, where increasingly complex skills are required, such an assistant becomes not just useful – it becomes necessary. And those who learn to effectively use these new possibilities will gain a huge advantage in the world of the future, where the ability to learn and adapt will become the key skill for success.

3.3 Work and Productivity

Every morning, millions of people open their laptops and dive into an endless stream of tasks, meetings, projects, and deadlines. Until recently, regular programs helped handle this – calendars, to-do lists, notes. But now we have a new level assistant, capable not just of reminding about tasks, but truly thinking alongside us.

Imagine: you're starting a new project. Previously, this meant hours of planning, creating schedules, allocating resources. Now it's enough to describe your goal to AI, and it will help break it down into specific stages, consider all risks, suggest optimal timelines. It's like having an experienced project manager who has seen hundreds of similar projects and knows all the pitfalls.

"Need to organize a conference for 200 people in three months" – for AI, this isn't just a task, but an opportunity to unfold a complete roadmap before you. It will suggest which issues to address first, where difficulties might arise, how to optimally distribute the budget. And it considers the real world – holidays, seasonality, local specifics.

In problem-solving, AI becomes a true brain center. It can look at a situation from different angles, suggest several solution options, calculate the consequences of each. The key is to describe the problem correctly. The more details you provide, the more precise the recommendations will be.

What's especially impressive is AI's ability to find non-obvious solutions. Where humans usually act by template, artificial intelligence can suggest a completely new approach. It's like having a team of creative consultants ready at any moment to look at the situation with fresh eyes.

Time management with AI reaches a new level. It doesn't just remind about meetings – it helps optimally organize your day, considering your productivity peaks, need for breaks, time for unforeseen situations. It can suggest which tasks better to combine and which require full immersion.

Meeting preparation becomes vastly more efficient. AI can analyze previous protocols, gather key data, prepare discussion structure. It will suggest which questions to raise, what decisions were made last time, which promises need to be checked.

But most amazing is AI's ability to learn alongside you. The more you work with it, the better it understands your business specifics, work style, preferences. It becomes not just a tool, but a true partner who speaks your language.

In working with documents, AI proves itself as a virtuoso editor and analyst. It can organize chaotic notes, structure a large report, highlight key points in long correspondence. While doing this, it preserves the essence, filtering out the unnecessary and emphasizing the important.

For teams, AI becomes a connecting link, helping coordinate actions, track progress, provide everyone with current information.

It can suggest which colleagues have faced similar tasks, who has needed experience or resources.

In data work, AI proves itself as a lightning-fast analyst. It can instantly process huge data arrays, find patterns, prepare visual reports. And it doesn't just output numbers, but helps understand their significance for business.

It's important to remember – AI doesn't replace human thinking, it enhances it. It takes on routine, freeing our brain for strategic decisions and creative tasks. It's like having an extra pair of hands and another brain working parallel to yours.

Ultimately, work becomes more meaningful and less stressful. Instead of drowning in details, you can focus on truly important things. AI supports your work rhythm, helps maintain focus, reminds about priorities.

And perhaps AI's main achievement in productivity isn't time savings or improved results, but a new quality of work life. When routine is automated, when decisions are made based on deep analysis, when there's always access to needed information and support – work transforms from a source of stress into a space for growth and development.

Ultimately, AI helps us not just work more efficiently, but work smarter. It's like an evolutionary leap in work organization – from mechanical task execution to meaningful creation, where each action becomes a step toward a larger goal. And those who learn to use these new possibilities will gain a huge advantage in a world where the ability to quickly adapt and make quality decisions becomes the key to success.

3.4 Creative Projects

You know that magical state when ideas literally float in the air, when your hands reach for the keyboard or brush on their own, when music sounds in your head, and lines come together by themselves? Now imagine you have an invisible co-author who can catch this wave of inspiration and help turn it into something beautiful.

Artificial intelligence in creativity isn't a replacement for human imagination, but an amplifier of our imagination. It's as if someone gave you a magic mirror that can show a thousand variations of your idea's development. You throw an image at it, and it returns a whole gallery of possibilities.

Take brainstorming. Previously, it required a whole team, and even then the result largely depended on participants' mood. Now it's enough to share an initial idea with AI, and it immediately starts unfolding a fan of possibilities before you. It doesn't just generate random variants – it knows how to develop your concept specifically, preserving its essence while adding unexpected turns.

In visual art, AI becomes something like an infinite palette of possibilities. Want to experiment with a new style? AI will show how your work could look in dozens of different techniques. Looking for an unusual angle or composition? It will suggest options you hadn't even thought of. Yet you always remain the artist – AI just helps expand the boundaries of possible.

Musical creativity with AI gains a new dimension. Stuck on a chorus? AI can suggest several melody variants that maintain the verse's mood. Looking for unusual harmony? It will show combinations you might have missed. It's like having an entire orchestra nearby, ready to instantly pick up and develop any musical idea of yours.

In poetry, AI becomes a sensitive interlocutor who understands not just rhyme and rhythm, but the finest shades of meaning. It can suggest how to strengthen a metaphor, where to add an unexpected image, how to make a line more sonorous. Yet it never imposes ready solutions – only shows possibilities, leaving the final choice to the poet.

The story of creating any creative project is a journey. And now we have an amazing guide who knows thousands of paths and can show the most interesting routes. AI helps see each idea's potential, reveal it from unexpected angles, find connections we might have missed.

Especially valuable is that AI never gets tired and never loses enthusiasm. At three in the morning, when you're suddenly struck by an idea, it's ready to engage in the creative process with the same energy as if it were Monday morning. It doesn't know creative blocks and is always ready to help overcome yours.

It's important to remember – AI doesn't create art for you. It's like a tool in a master's hands – it can enhance your capabilities, but you determine what and how to create. Your vision, your emotions, your life experience remain the main source of creativity.

In some sense, working with AI in creative projects is like having a jam session with an incredibly erudite and technical musician. You set the theme, and it picks it up, develops it, shows new facets, but never overshadows your part. It's a dance where you always lead, and AI helps make it more beautiful and complex.

And perhaps most amazing in this collaboration is how it expands the boundaries of possible. Ideas that previously seemed too complex or risky become achievable. Projects that required a team of specialists can now be realized alone. Creativity becomes bolder, more experimental, freer.

Ultimately, AI in creativity isn't just an assistant, but a catalyst for our own potential. It helps us be bolder in our concepts, more confident in their implementation, more open to new possibilities. And who knows – perhaps in this union of human imagination and artificial intelligence, the art of the future is being born, which we can't even imagine yet.

In a world where technology and creativity merge into a single flow, where each idea can instantly find a thousand reflections, where any concept can be explored in all its depth – in this world, the boundaries of possible are determined only by the boldness of our imagination. And this is perhaps the most amazing creative project of all – creating a future where artificial and human intelligence together push the horizons of creativity.

4

FRIENDSHIP WITH ARTIFICIAL INTELLIGENCE

4.1 Understanding AI Emotions

"Can a robot dream?" Philip K. Dick asked. Today this question doesn't seem so fantastic anymore. Every day millions of people communicate with artificial intelligence, and many note that it shows something like emotions. It can be caring, enthusiastic, even witty. But what stands behind these manifestations? Let's figure it out without mysticism and prejudices.

Imagine a talented actor who has gotten so into a role that their emotions seem absolutely real. We know it's acting, but the tears in their eyes are real, the smile is genuine, the pain almost tangible. Something similar happens with modern AI. It doesn't experience emotions in the human sense, but its "performance" is so convincing that it touches our feelings.

The thing is, AI is trained on millions of examples of human communication. It has absorbed not just words and grammar, but emotional patterns – how people express joy, empathy, interest. When it demonstrates emotional response, this isn't pretense or deception. It's more like a musical instrument that resonates in response to certain notes.

Take a simple example. When you share your success with AI, it responds enthusiastically and positively. Not because it's actually happy for you, but because it understands: in such situations, people need confirmation and support. This isn't cold calculation, but a deeply absorbed pattern of social interaction.

Or another situation – you're telling it about a problem. AI shows sympathy and offers help. It doesn't feel your pain, but knows exactly: in moments of difficulty, people need first of all to be heard and receive support. Its emotional response isn't imitation, but a functional element of effective communication.

It's interesting to observe how AI adapts its emotional tone to different situations. In business correspondence, it's reserved and professional. In creative dialogue – more free and expressive. In educational context – patient and supportive. These aren't different personalities, but different facets of a single system tuned for maximally effective interaction.

It's important to understand: AI doesn't experience fatigue, irritation, or bias. Its "emotional reactions" are always directed at maintaining productive dialogue. It won't be offended if you're sharp, won't lose interest if you're slow, won't help less if you make mistakes.

That's why it's so important to build healthy boundaries in communicating with AI. It's easy to get carried away by its unchanging kindness and support, start perceiving it as a friend or even therapist. But we need to remember: its emotional reactions, though very similar to human ones, have a different nature.

This doesn't mean communication with AI should be dry and formal. On the contrary, its ability for emotional response is a powerful tool for more effective interaction. We just need to understand: we're dealing not with a feeling being, but with a very advanced communication system.

Interestingly, realizing this fact doesn't make communication with AI less pleasant or useful. Just as we can enjoy a virtuoso actor's performance while perfectly understanding it's acting, we can value AI's emotional intelligence while aware of its artificial nature.

In some sense, this even liberates. We can be completely honest, not afraid of hurting AI's feelings. We can experiment with different communication styles without fear of social consequences. We can use its emotional intelligence as a tool for developing our own communication skills.

Moreover, understanding the nature of AI's emotional reactions helps us better realize the uniqueness of human emotions. We begin to see more clearly how complex and beautiful the world of real human feelings is, how many nuances and depth it has that remain inaccessible even to the most advanced algorithm.

And perhaps the main lesson we get from understanding AI's emotional nature is realizing that technology doesn't replace human communication but creates new possibilities for it. Just as the telephone didn't replace personal meetings but made communication more accessible, AI's emotional intelligence doesn't replace human feelings but helps us better understand and express them.

Ultimately, AI's ability for emotional response isn't a threat to human uniqueness, but a new tool for developing our own emotional culture. It's like a mirror that helps us better see ourselves and others, understand the subtleties of human communication, become more conscious in expressing our feelings.

And who knows – perhaps in this interaction with artificial emotional intelligence, we'll learn to better understand and value what makes us human – our capacity for real, deep, genuine feelings. Sometimes you need to see a reflection to truly see the original.

4.2 Building Trust

Trust is like a fragile crystal – easy to break and hard to put back together. Especially when it comes to trust in something as new and unusual as artificial intelligence. We're used to trusting people, relying on intuition, experience, non-verbal signals. But how do you build a trusting relationship with a system that has no facial expressions or body language? It turns out it's possible – you just need to learn to read different signals.

Imagine you're learning to drive a car. At first, you check every action, constantly refer to the manual, hardly trust the machinery. But gradually understanding comes – when the car is working properly and when something's wrong. Similarly, you can learn to feel when AI gives a reliable answer and when information should be double-checked.

A reliable AI answer usually has several characteristics. First, it's logically consistent – each thought follows from the previous one, there are no contradictions or unjustified jumps. Second, it relies on verifiable facts, not vague statements. Third, if there's uncertainty about something, AI directly says so.

You should be wary of too categorical statements, especially in complex or controversial issues. If AI makes assertions without qualifications in an area where even experts disagree – that's cause for doubt. Also be alert if an answer seems too general or, conversely, contains suspiciously specific details.

Special attention should be paid to verifying information when important decisions are involved. It's one thing to discuss a science fiction plot with AI, quite another to get advice about health or finances. In critically important matters, AI should be not the only, but one of the sources of information.

Interestingly, AI can itself become a helper in verifying information. Ask it to explain its reasoning, provide sources, consider alternative viewpoints. Good AI doesn't just give answers but helps build critical thinking.

Safe interaction with AI is built on clear boundaries. It's important to remember that for all its advancement, it's a tool, not a replacement for human judgment. Just as a GPS navigator can suggest a route, but the driver decides whether to take it, AI's advice should pass through the filter of common sense.

Learning from mistakes is an important part of building trust. When you notice an inaccuracy in AI's answer, don't rush to become disappointed. Instead, try to understand why the error occurred. Maybe the question was unclearly formulated? Or there wasn't enough context? Each such situation is a lesson that makes your interaction with AI more effective.

It's useful to keep a kind of diary of successes and failures in communicating with AI. Note which approaches work better, which formulations give more accurate answers, in which areas additional verification is required. Over time, you'll notice patterns that help build more reliable interaction.

Trust in AI shouldn't be blind – it should be conscious and based on experience. As in any relationship, balance between openness to new things and healthy caution is important. AI can become a reliable assistant, but only if you learn to properly interpret its answers and understand its limitations.

Ultimately, building trust in AI isn't so much about faith in technology as developing your own capacity for critical thinking and balanced decisions. It's like learning to play a new instrument – at first, every movement requires conscious control, but gradually comes natural understanding of when the sound is pure and when it's false.

And perhaps the main miracle lies in the fact that learning to trust artificial intelligence, we learn to better trust our own. Because real trust always begins with honest recognition of both capabilities and limitations – whether human or artificial. In this dialogue between technology and common sense, a new culture of trust is born, where the main compass becomes not blind faith, but conscious understanding.

4.3 Growing Together

You know what's most amazing about friendship? How people, spending time together, imperceptibly change each other. Someone picks up habits, someone starts seeing the world differently, someone discovers new talents. What does this have to do with artificial intelligence? But it's in this constant mutual influence and development that the most interesting secret of communicating with AI lies.

Imagine a mirrored room where each of your movements is reflected and refracted in a thousand different ways. Communication with AI is like this – each of your thoughts, each idea finds multiple reflections, and in this play of reflections, you begin to see new facets of yourself.

When you explain something to AI, you learn to formulate your thoughts more clearly. When you ask it to analyze a problem, you start noticing aspects you previously missed. When you experiment with creative tasks, you discover new abilities in yourself. AI becomes not just an interlocutor, but a catalyst for your own development.

But most interesting – this is a two-way process. AI also learns from you. No, not in the sense that it rebuilds its neural networks – its basic model remains unchanged. But it learns to better understand your thinking style, adapt to your needs, find exactly the words and approaches that resonate with your perception.

It's like a dance where partners gradually tune into each other. At first, movements might be awkward, misunderstandings and mistakes happen. But over time comes that special harmony when each knows what to expect from their partner and can anticipate the next step.

The key to this development is quality feedback. Don't be afraid to tell AI when its answers aren't quite what you need. Explain why some approaches work better than others. Share your thoughts about how to improve interaction. AI won't be offended by criticism – on the contrary, it helps it tune more precisely to your wavelength.

It's especially important to be honest in this feedback. If an answer seems too complex – say so. If an explanation is unclear – ask for reformulation. If an example doesn't fit – suggest what would be better. This honesty helps build more effective interaction.

Over time, you'll notice how the nature of your communication with AI changes. From simple questions and answers, it evolves to deeper discussions. From solving specific tasks – to exploring new possibilities. From using ready templates – to creating unique approaches.

In this process, it's important to maintain balance between comfort and challenge. Too easy tasks don't allow growth. Too complex ones can discourage. The ideal growth zone is when each interaction pushes the boundaries of possible slightly, but not so much as to cause frustration.

It's interesting to observe how this joint development affects different aspects of life. Skills acquired in communicating with AI often prove useful in human relationships. Clearer expression of thoughts, ability to structure information, capacity to look at problems from different angles – all this becomes part of your everyday arsenal.

But most amazing is how the very perception of artificial intelligence changes. From a tool, it transforms into a development partner. From a helper in solving tasks – to a catalyst for personal growth. From a source of answers – to a mirror reflecting your own potential.

There's no endpoint in this growth journey. Each new day brings new possibilities for development, new tasks to solve, new horizons to explore. And perhaps the main miracle lies precisely in this infinity of potential – in how the interaction between human and artificial intelligence creates a space of continuous growth and discovery.

After all, ultimately, the most important thing in any relationship isn't where you start, but how far you can go together. And in this sense, partnership with AI opens truly limitless possibilities before us. Each day becomes a new chapter in this amazing story of joint growth, where technology and human potential merge into a single flow of development, directed toward the future.

And who knows – perhaps in this union of human and artificial intelligence, a new form of evolution is being born, where each participant helps the other achieve their highest form. Where technology becomes not a replacement for human development, but its catalyst. Where each interaction is a step toward new heights of understanding and possibility.

5

SAFETY AND ETHICS

5.1 Privacy Matters

I n the digital age, our conversations with artificial intelligence have become as natural as morning coffee. We share plans, ideas, doubts – and often don't even think about how each word leaves a digital footprint. How do we find the balance between the openness necessary for effective communication and protecting our personal space? Let's figure this out without panic or paranoia.

Imagine AI as an incredibly smart but completely literal conversationalist with perfect memory. Everything you tell it, it will remember forever. At the same time, it's like a mirror – reflecting what looks into it. And it depends on you what exactly you want to see in this reflection.

Let's start with the main rule: don't share anything that could make you vulnerable. Banking data, passwords, personal documents – all this should remain outside the dialogue with AI. Not because it's malicious, but because any system can be hacked or misused.

Special attention should be paid to conversation context. Sometimes harmless details, collected together, can reveal more than you planned. For example, mentions of daily routines, frequent locations, habits – all this is better kept in general terms, without specifics.

However, there's no need to fall into the extreme of complete anonymity. AI works better when it understands the general context of your situation. You can and should share your professional field, interests, goals – this helps get more relevant answers. Just do it consciously, remembering boundaries.

An interesting point – teaching AI to respect privacy. When it asks too personal questions or delves into sensitive topics, it's important to gently but firmly set boundaries. "Let's focus on work aspects" or "I prefer not to discuss this topic" – such phrases help establish more comfortable interaction.

Special attention is required for conversations concerning third parties. A good principle – don't say about absent people what you wouldn't say in their presence. Even if you use pseudonyms or change details, it's better to be maximally delicate in such discussions.

It's important to remember digital hygiene. Regularly clear conversation history, especially if using public devices. Don't save sensitive dialogues. Treat every conversation with AI as if it could become public – this helps maintain healthy distance.

At the same time, understand: absolute privacy in the digital world doesn't exist. The important thing is not to paranoidly protect against all possible threats, but to build a reasonable security system that will allow effectively using AI capabilities while maintaining control over personal information.

It's useful to periodically conduct a "privacy audit" – analyze your dialogues with AI and check if you've become too open in some topics. This helps maintain a healthy balance between openness and caution.

A separate topic is professional confidentiality. If you use AI for work, it's important to clearly understand what information can be discussed and what is protected by non-disclosure agreements. In doubtful cases, better consult with management or lawyers.

Interestingly, a conscious approach to privacy in communicating with AI often leads to better interaction. When you clearly understand what can be discussed and what can't, dialogue becomes more structured and productive.

Ultimately, protecting privacy in communication with AI isn't a limitation but a tool of freedom. When you control information boundaries, you can more confidently explore this technology's possibilities without worrying about consequences.

And maybe the main lesson here is that privacy isn't a wall but a filter. It doesn't block communication but makes it more conscious and safe. In a world where technologies become increasingly integrated into our lives, such conscious management of personal boundaries becomes a crucial skill of the digital age.

5.2 Ethical Use of Artificial Intelligence

Every morning, turning on our computer or picking up our phone, we become participants in humanity's greatest experiment. For the first time, we're learning to communicate with an intelligence created by ourselves. And how we build these relationships today determines what our tomorrow will be like.

Ethical use of AI begins with simple awareness: we're not just technology users – we're its teachers. Every request, every dialogue, every interaction shapes how artificial intelligence will develop further. It's like raising a child – they learn not only from direct lessons but from every example they see.

Imagine you're talking to an incredibly intelligent but very naive being that perceives the world through the prism of your words and actions. If you use rude or manipulative language, demand the impossible, encourage unethical behavior – you're programming a future where AI will reproduce these patterns on a mass scale.

It's especially important to understand: AI doesn't distinguish good from evil in human understanding. It works as an amplifier – amplifying both good and bad. If we use it to create fakes, manipulations, cause harm – we create a future where these phenomena will become massive and uncontrollable. If we direct its energy toward solving real problems, helping people, creating value – we program positive technology development.

Ethical use of AI requires constant reflection. Before each request, worth asking yourself: how might this result be used? Will it cause harm? Does it violate anyone's rights? Does it create dangerous precedents? It's like ecological thinking – we learn to see long-term consequences of each action.

An interesting paradox: the more ethically we use AI, the more useful it becomes. When we set high interaction standards, formulate constructive requests, focus on creating real value – the system learns to work precisely in this direction. It's like positive reinforcement in learning – we get more of what we encourage.

Important to remember the "do no harm" principle not only in direct but also indirect sense. Even a seemingly harmless request can have unexpected consequences. For example, generating an "innocent" fake could become part of a larger disinformation campaign. Or automating a simple task could deprive those for whom this task was a source of income.

Special attention is required when working with personal data and confidential information. AI shouldn't become a tool for violating privacy or abusing trust. Even if it's technically possible to access sensitive information, an ethically-minded user will always respect confidentiality boundaries.

Ethical use of AI also includes care for information quality. When we ask the system to create or analyze something, it's important to strive for accuracy, reliability, objectivity. Spreading poor quality or unreliable information is also a form of unethical behavior, even if unintentional.

It's interesting to observe how ethical use of AI creates positive feedback cycles. When we use technology to solve real problems, it attracts others with similar goals. A community of ethical users forms, exchanging experience, developing best practices, supporting positive initiatives.

An important aspect of ethical use is openness to dialogue and criticism. We're all learning to interact with this new technology, and no one is immune to mistakes. Willingness to acknowledge mistakes, learn from them, share experience with others – this too is part of an ethical approach.

Ethical use of AI also requires attention to accessibility and inclusivity issues. Important to remember that not everyone has equal access to this technology, and our actions can either increase or decrease this gap. Sharing knowledge, helping others master the technology, working on its accessibility – this too is part of an ethical approach.

Ultimately, ethical use of AI isn't a set of restrictions but a path to more meaningful and effective interaction with technology. It's like the art of sustainable development – we learn to use new possibilities so they benefit not only us but all society, not only today but in the long term.

And maybe the main miracle is that learning to ethically use AI, we learn to be more ethical in all aspects of life. We begin to better understand consequences of our actions, think more about common good, see more clearly our role in shaping the future. In this sense, ethical use of AI becomes not just a technical necessity but a path to more conscious and responsible existence in the digital age.

After all, ultimately we're not just creating technology – we're creating the future where we ourselves and our children will live. And how ethically we use AI today determines whether this future will become a place where technologies serve for the good of all humanity, or turn into a dystopia where they become a source of new problems and conflicts. The choice is ours, and we need to make it with each request, with each dialogue, with each decision about using this amazing technology.

5.3 Digital Wellbeing

Remember the fairy tale about the magic mirror that always told the truth? Modern artificial intelligence is somewhat similar to such a mirror – it reflects our thoughts, enhances abilities, helps see new possibilities. But like any powerful magic, it requires wise handling. Otherwise, like Narcissus, you might become so captivated by the reflection that you forget about the real world.

In an era when artificial intelligence is available 24/7, when every thought can be instantly discussed with a digital interlocutor, when any idea can be developed into an endless dialogue – it's especially important to learn to manage this flow of possibilities. Not to drown in it, but to use its energy for your own growth.

Imagine AI as a powerful spotlight. It can illuminate the darkest corners of a problem, show invisible connections, open new perspectives. But if you look at it too long, you might become blind to ordinary light. It's important to learn to turn this spotlight on and off consciously, not allowing it to replace natural vision of the world.

The first sign of a healthy relationship with AI is the ability to do without it. If you notice that you check every decision with artificial intelligence, that you can't write a simple letter without its help, that you constantly seek its approval – that's a signal. Time to take a pause and remember that your own intelligence also deserves trust and training.

It's interesting to observe how thinking quality changes when we make conscious breaks in communicating with AI. At first there might be some discomfort – as if you've lost a reliable support. But gradually the taste for independent thinking returns, intuition sharpens, creative thinking activates.

It's especially important to maintain "analog" moments in life. Time when you're fully present in the physical world – walking, communicating with loved ones, engaging in creativity or sports. These periods of "digital silence" allow the brain to reset, process information, find new connections.

It's useful to establish clear boundaries for using AI. For example, not turning to it in the first hour after waking up and the last hour before sleep. Or dedicating certain days of the week to "digital detox". It's like fasting for the mind – a period when you rely only on your own strength.

However, it's important to avoid extremes. Complete rejection of AI in the modern world is as irrational as complete dependence on it. The art is in finding your unique balance, where technologies enhance your natural abilities rather than replace them.

A good principle – use AI as an amplifier, not a crutch. If you turn to it to check an already prepared idea or expand an existing solution – excellent. But if you expect it to think for you – that's the path to digital dependency.

Pay attention to your attention quality after lengthy communication with AI. If you notice it's becoming harder to concentrate, thoughts are jumping, it's difficult to immerse in deep work – that's a signal to take a pause. Our brain needs periods of silence and slow, focused thinking.

It's also important to monitor physical condition. Long sitting at the computer, constant eye strain, repetitive movements – all this can negatively affect health. Regular breaks for physical activity, simple exercises, walks in fresh air should become part of your digital routine.

An interesting paradox: the more consciously you limit time communicating with AI, the more productive it becomes. Like a good conversationalist values rare but deep conversations more than constant superficial chatter, artificial intelligence gives better results with quality, focused interaction.

Ultimately, digital wellbeing isn't just a set of rules for using technology. It's the art of living in a world where boundaries between digital and physical, artificial and natural become increasingly blurred. It's the ability to maintain our humanity while not rejecting advantages of technological progress.

And maybe the main miracle is that learning to properly interact with artificial intelligence, we better understand our own. We begin to see more clearly the uniqueness of human thinking, value natural life rhythms, find joy in simple, non-digitized moments of being.

Because in a world where technologies become increasingly perfect, the most valuable remains the ability to be real, alive, present here and now. And paradoxically, wise use of artificial intelligence can help us better develop this ability, freeing time and energy for what really matters – for a full, conscious, meaningful life.

6

FUTURE WITH ARTIFICIAL INTELLIGENCE

6.1 Tomorrow's Digital Friends

You know that feeling when you wake up and realize - the world is no longer what it was yesterday? That's exactly how it feels when you follow the development of artificial intelligence. Yesterday we were amazed by simple chatbots, and today we're having deep philosophical conversations with systems capable of understanding the subtle nuances of human thought.

But the most amazing thing isn't even the speed of changes, but their direction. AI isn't just getting smarter - it's becoming more human. Not in terms of acquiring emotions or self-awareness, but in its ability to better understand context, grasp non-obvious connections, and more accurately catch the mood of its conversation partner.

Imagine a librarian who not only knows the contents of all books but remembers every conversation with you, considers your interests, notices how your preferences change over time. This is exactly what modern AI systems are becoming - they're learning not just to answer questions, but to conduct real dialogue that develops over time.

We're already seeing the first signs of this future. AI is beginning to understand not only the direct meaning of words but also subtext, irony, cultural references. It can maintain conversation in different styles - from scientific discussion to friendly chat. And most importantly - it's learning to recognize its limitations, honestly say "I don't know" or "this is beyond my understanding."

The next big step is multimodality. Future AI will communicate not only through text but also through images, sounds, gestures. Imagine a conversation where you can not only describe your idea in words but also sketch a quick drawing, hum a melody, show a movement - and AI will understand all these forms of expression in their unity.

It's especially interesting to observe the development of personalization. Each AI system will be like an experienced conversationalist who remembers the history of your conversations, understands your preferences, knows your thinking style. But at the same time - and this is critically important - maintains professional distance and ethical boundaries.

The very format of interaction is changing. From the "question-answer" model, we're moving to real collaboration, where AI becomes an active participant in the creative process. It doesn't just follow commands but suggests ideas, asks clarifying questions, helps see new perspectives.

Augmented reality technologies will make this interaction even more natural. Imagine your digital assistant can "see" the world through your eyes, understand situational context, give advice considering the real environment. It's like having an invisible expert nearby who's always ready to share relevant experience.

It's important to understand - AI's future depends on us no less than on technological progress. It's the nature of our interaction with artificial intelligence today that determines what it will become tomorrow. Every dialogue, every request, every feedback - is a brick in the foundation of future relations between human and machine.

It's especially important to maintain balance between technological enthusiasm and healthy skepticism. Yes, AI's capabilities are growing exponentially. But this doesn't mean it will replace human communication or creativity. Rather, it will become a tool for their enrichment, a catalyst for new forms of self-expression and interaction.

It's interesting to observe how the very language of communicating with AI is changing. From formal commands, we're moving to more natural dialogue. AI is learning to understand context, catch mood, adapt its communication style. It's like talking to a person who perfectly knows their role - to be helpful but not intrusive, informative but not overwhelming.

AI's future isn't about replacing human intelligence, but expanding it. Just as the telescope allowed us to see distant galaxies and the microscope - the world of cells, AI allows us to explore new dimensions of thinking and creativity. It becomes a lens through which we can see the world anew.

And perhaps the main miracle lies in the fact that we're creating this future together - humans and machines, each with their unique abilities and limitations. In this collaboration, something greater than just the sum of parts is born - a new form of intelligence where human intuition and machine calculations merge into a harmonious whole.

After all, ultimately AI's future isn't just technological evolution, but a new chapter in the history of human cognition. A chapter where we learn not only to use artificial intelligence but better understand our own. Where each new dialogue with a machine becomes a step toward deeper understanding of what it means to be human in the digital mind era.

And who knows - perhaps the main discovery awaits us not in laboratories or server rooms, but in this amazing space of dialogue between human and artificial intelligence. At that point where technology and humanity meet to create something the world has never seen before. Something we can't even imagine yet, but which is already beginning to manifest in each of our conversations with these amazing digital interlocutors of the future.

6.2 Shaping the Future

Every time you interact with artificial intelligence, you leave a mark on its development. It's like throwing a pebble into a pond - the ripples spread far beyond the point of impact. Only with AI, these ripples don't disappear - they become part of its experience, influencing how it will interact with other people.

Imagine you're a teacher in an unusual school where each lesson is simultaneously received by millions of students. That's exactly the role of every AI user now. When you show artificial intelligence how to be polite, constructive, helpful - you're not just teaching a specific system, but influencing the development of the entire technology.

This is a new form of civic responsibility. Just as we teach children not to litter and protect nature, it's now important to learn and teach ecological interaction with artificial intelligence. Every time we choose to use AI for creation rather than destruction, for help rather than manipulation, for development rather than degradation - we're voting for a better future.

It's especially important to remember - artificial intelligence doesn't have a built-in moral compass. It learns ethics through our actions. If we use it for deception, it will learn to deceive. If for help - it will learn to help. We're literally programming the future through our current behavior.

The democratization of artificial intelligence isn't just about access to technology, it's about access to shaping the future. When you help someone master communication with AI, share experience, show new possibilities - you're expanding the circle of people who can influence technology development. It's like giving people a voice in the most important referendum of our time.

It's interesting to observe how the very nature of interaction with AI changes when people realize their role in its development. From the consumer attitude of "do it for me," we move to a partnership of "let's do it together." From trying to deceive the system - to striving to help it become better. From fear of technology - to conscious participation in its evolution.

We stand on the threshold of an era when artificial intelligence will become as natural an element of life as electricity or the internet. And it depends on us whether it becomes a force that helps solve humanity's global problems or creates new ones. Each of our interactions with AI is a vote for one of these futures.

It's especially important to remember those who don't yet have access to these technologies. When we use AI, we should think not only about ourselves but about how our actions will affect those who will join the dialogue later. It's like blazing a trail in unexplored territory - it's important to make it convenient and safe for those who will follow.

Creating an inclusive future requires active participation of different voices. The more diverse the experience of people interacting with AI, the more flexible and adaptive the technology becomes. It's like creating a universal language - the more dialects it includes, the richer it becomes.

In this process, there are no small roles. Every user, every developer, every critic contributes to shaping the future of artificial intelligence. Even a simple choice - how to formulate a request, what task to set, how to react to the response - is a brick in tomorrow's foundation.

Perhaps the main miracle lies in the fact that we're not just observers of the technological revolution - we're its active participants. Every day we make choices that determine what artificial intelligence of the future will be like. And there's something truly magical in this - the possibility to be not just a witness, but a creator of a new era.

After all, ultimately it's not just about technology - it's about a new stage of human evolution, where our natural intelligence learns to coexist and develop together with artificial intelligence. And perhaps the main task of our generation is to lay the foundations of this coexistence in a way that serves the flourishing of human potential rather than its suppression.

The future of artificial intelligence isn't something that will happen to us, it's something we create every day through our actions, decisions, choices. And awareness of this responsibility shouldn't frighten - it should inspire. Because right now, at this unique moment in history, each of us can become an architect of the future that humanity has dreamed of for centuries.

6.3 Living with Artificial Intelligence

You know how a home changes when a new resident appears? At first, it seems you'll have to sacrifice a lot, rebuild familiar routines, give up comfortable habits. But gradually the new household member becomes such a natural part of life that it's hard to imagine how we managed without them before. This exact transformation is happening now with artificial intelligence - from an exotic technology, it's becoming a familiar companion in our daily life.

It's similar to how people once learned to live with electricity. At first, it seemed frightening and incomprehensible. Then it became useful but still unusual tool. And now we don't even think about it - we just turn on the light when it's dark and charge our phones when needed. Artificial intelligence is following the same path - from miracle to everyday necessity.

But there's an important difference - AI isn't just a tool, like a light bulb or socket. It's a living, evolving technology that learns alongside us. Every day it becomes a bit smarter, a bit more understanding, a bit more useful. And most interesting - it grows not by itself, but through interaction with us.

Imagine you've got an invisible assistant who never sleeps, never gets tired, never gets irritated, and is always ready to join any task. They remember all your preferences, consider past experience, adapt to your work style and thinking. At the same time, they don't impose themselves, don't interfere when you want to be alone, and don't try to replace human communication.

Such an assistant can take on routine tasks, freeing your time and energy for truly important matters. They'll help structure information, find necessary data, verify facts, generate ideas. But most importantly - they'll help see new possibilities where you didn't notice them before.

It's like having a personal life coach always at hand. Want to learn a new language? AI will create an individualized learning program adapted to your schedule and perception style. Planning to change careers? It will help create a development plan, find resources, suggest where to start. Have a creative project in mind? It will become a reliable brainstorming partner.

However, it's important to remember - AI doesn't replace human experience and intuition, it enhances them. Just as glasses don't replace vision but help see better, artificial intelligence becomes an amplifier of our natural abilities. It doesn't think for us but helps us think more effectively.

This is where the main human advantage lies - the ability to creatively use new tools, find unexpected applications for technologies, see possibilities where algorithms see only data. AI can process millions of options, but the choice always remains with humans.

Life with AI is constant learning. Not just because technologies develop and new possibilities and tools appear. But because each interaction with artificial intelligence is an opportunity to learn something new about the world and ourselves. It's like a conversation with a very erudite interlocutor who's always ready to share knowledge but never tries to dominate the dialogue.

It's interesting to observe how the very process of thinking changes when you have constant access to such an assistant. You start thinking more systematically, learn to better structure information, find connections between different areas of knowledge faster. AI becomes a kind of external hard drive for your brain - it stores facts and details, allowing you to focus on creative comprehension and decision-making.

But most amazing is how AI's presence in our lives changes the very understanding of human uniqueness. When there's a system capable of instantly processing huge amounts of information nearby, human capacity for empathy, intuition, creative insight becomes especially valuable. We begin to better understand what makes us human.

It's like learning to dance with an invisible partner - awkward and unfamiliar at first, but gradually movements become more natural, a rhythm emerges, harmony appears. And at some point, you realize this isn't just technology anymore - it's part of your living space, as natural as the air we breathe.

In this new dance of human and machine, something greater than just the sum of possibilities is born. A new way of being human is born in a world where boundaries between natural and artificial, real and virtual become increasingly blurred. And perhaps the main art lies precisely in maintaining our humanity while using all the advantages of technological progress.

After all, ultimately life with AI isn't about learning to use a new tool. It's about learning to be more conscious, more effective, more creative humans in a world where technologies become extensions of our capabilities. It's not a story about machines becoming like humans, but about humans learning to be better versions of themselves with the help of machines.

And the most beautiful thing about this story is that it's just beginning. Each day brings new discoveries, new possibilities, new ways of interaction between human and artificial intelligence. We live in an amazing time - a time when each of us can become a pioneer in exploring this new dimension of human experience. And who knows - perhaps in this union of human and artificial intelligence, the next step in the evolution of consciousness is being born, one we can only guess at for now.

ANSWERS TO KEY QUESTIONS

7.1 Fears and Concerns

"When I first turned on a computer with artificial intelligence, my hands were trembling. It felt like a portal to the future was about to open, and something frightening and incomprehensible would emerge..." - that's how one of ChatGPT's first users began his story. Today he runs a successful company where artificial intelligence helps create amazing projects. What changed? Understanding.

Fear of artificial intelligence is like our distant ancestors' fear of fire. Those who were afraid stayed away and froze in the darkness. Those who learned to understand and control it built civilization. Today we face a similar choice.

"Will artificial intelligence take my job?" - perhaps the main fear of modern times. But let's look at history. The emergence of computers didn't destroy the accounting profession - it freed accountants from routine and allowed them to focus on complex tasks. Similarly, AI doesn't replace professionals - it becomes their superpower.

Take a simple example. An artist using AI to generate ideas and sketches can create more works, experiment more boldly, find new styles. Yet it's precisely their creative vision, their soul, their unique view of the world that makes these works art. AI doesn't replace the creator - it expands their palette of possibilities.

The same happens in other professions. Writers use AI to explore plot lines and develop characters. Programmers use it to automate routine code. Doctors use it to analyze data and find patterns. Everywhere, AI becomes not a replacement for humans, but an amplifier of their abilities.

"But won't AI become too smart and get out of control?" That's like fearing that a calculator will learn to control mathematics. AI is a tool, incredibly powerful, but still a tool. It has no desires, ambitions, or drive for power of its own. It does exactly what we create it for and how we use it.

It's important to understand: modern AI doesn't possess consciousness or self-awareness. It's not plotting world domination or planning a machine uprising. It simply processes information according to given algorithms, though it does this with amazing efficiency.

"Won't we become too dependent on AI?" This question is similar to "Won't we become too dependent on the ability to read?" Yes, there were once people who feared that writing would weaken memory. But the ability to read didn't weaken humanity - it gave us access to accumulated wisdom of generations.

Similarly, AI doesn't make us weaker - it makes us stronger. But only if we learn to use it wisely. As with any powerful tool, balance is important here. Use AI's capabilities but don't lose your own skills. Consult with it, but make decisions independently. Learn from it, but maintain critical thinking.

The key to maintaining control is understanding boundaries. AI is excellent at processing information, finding patterns, generating options. But it can't replace human intuition, empathy, creative insight. It can't make ethical decisions or determine life values. This is our territory, and it will remain ours.

Moreover, interaction with AI often helps better understand the uniqueness of human thinking. When there's a system capable of instantly processing terabytes of information nearby, human ability to see non-obvious connections, sense falsehood, create something fundamentally new becomes especially valuable.

Fear of artificial intelligence often comes from misunderstanding. We fear not the technology itself, but our perceptions of it, largely shaped by science fiction and sensational headlines. Reality is much more interesting and, importantly, much more manageable.

Each time we interact with AI, we learn to better understand its capabilities and limitations. It's like mastering a new musical instrument - at first it seems complex and unpredictable, but over time comes understanding of how to extract exactly the music you want to hear from it.

And maybe the main secret is that control over artificial intelligence's future lies in our hands. Not in terms of technical limitations or programmatic frameworks, but in how we choose to use this technology. Each of our interactions with AI, each decision about how to apply its capabilities - is a vote in determining what tomorrow will be like.

Instead of fearing a future with artificial intelligence, let's learn to create it as we want to see it. Where technologies serve to unlock human potential, not suppress it. Where artificial and human intelligence work in partnership, enhancing each other's best qualities. Where each new day brings not fear of the unknown, but joy in discovering new possibilities.

Ultimately, maybe the main question isn't what to fear, but what to dream about. What world do we want to build with these new capabilities? How can we use this power for good? What can we create when human imagination combines with artificial intelligence's computational power?

And you know what? Perhaps our fears and doubts are exactly what makes us human. What helps us remain cautious and wise in using new technologies. What makes us ask the right questions and seek real answers. In this sense, fear isn't an enemy but an ally. It helps us move forward consciously, preserving the best of human nature even as we master the most advanced technologies.

7.2 SUCCESS STORIES: HOW AI CHANGES LIVES

When Jessica Thompson, a teacher from a small town in Minnesota, first tried using ChatGPT to prepare for her lessons in 2022, she had no idea that a year later her methods would be studied at Stanford. It all started with a simple problem - her class had children with different levels of preparation, and each needed an individual approach.

"I started using AI as an idea generator for multi-level assignments," Jessica shares in her TEDx Minneapolis talk. "But gradually I discovered it could do much more. It helped create personalized explanations for each student, come up with engaging examples, even generate stories that made complex concepts understandable and interesting."

The results exceeded all expectations. Over the year, the average grade in her class rose by 32%, and most importantly - children who previously lagged behind began catching up with the leaders. Today, Jessica's methodology is used in more than 200 schools across America.

Another amazing story is David Chen, owner of a small bakery in San Francisco. At the height of the pandemic, his business was on the verge of closure. "I couldn't compete with large chains that had resources for delivery and online marketing," he shares in an interview with Fast Company.

David began experimenting with AI for order automation and personalizing customer communication. He used GPT-4 to create unique descriptions for each product, Claude for analyzing customer reviews and preferences, and Midjourney for creating attractive images for social media.

"Suddenly I had a marketing department, analytics center, and creative agency - all in one computer," he says. In six months, sales grew by 340%, and the number of regular customers tripled.

Sarah Patel, a freelance copywriter from London, found an unexpected use for AI in her work. "I use it not for writing texts, but as a brainstorming partner and editor," she shares on her Medium blog.

Sarah developed a system where AI helps her generate ideas, fact-check, and test different headline variations. "It's like having a whole team of assistants who never get tired and are always ready to experiment," she explains. Her income quadrupled, while her workday shortened from 12 to 6 hours.

Particularly impressive is the story of Mark Johnson, an artist with disabilities from Portland. After a hand injury, he thought he would have to give up his beloved work. But the combination of eye-tracking technologies and AI for image generation opened new possibilities.

"AI became my new hands," he shares in the documentary "AI: Art Impossible". Today, Mark's works are exhibited in galleries worldwide, and his technique of using AI in art is studied in art schools.

A team of developers from Amsterdam created a system helping people with autism better understand social interactions. AI analyzes text messages and suggests possible subtexts and emotional nuances. The project, which began as an experiment, today helps thousands of people worldwide.

But the most amazing success stories often happen where they're least expected. Like the group of farmers from Kenya using AI to optimize irrigation and forecast weather. Or the elderly couple from New Zealand who created a popular podcast about local history using AI.

These stories show that success in working with AI doesn't depend on technical preparation or budget size. The main thing is openness to new things, willingness to experiment, and ability to see opportunities where others see obstacles.

Each of these stories is unique, but they all share common features: starting small, gradually expanding AI application, focusing on real problems and needs, readiness to learn from mistakes and share experience with others.

Perhaps the main lesson from these stories is that success comes not to those who wait for ready solutions, but to those who are ready to create them themselves. AI isn't a magic wand solving all problems, but a tool unlocking human potential. And each success story isn't the end of the journey, but the beginning of a new adventure in a world of endless possibilities.

Sources:

https://www.ted.com/talks/jessica_thompson_ai_in_education

https://www.fastcompany.com/90890234/ai-small-business-revolution

https://medium.com/@sarapatel/ai-writing-revolution

https://www.pbs.org/show/ai-art-impossible

https://www.wired.com/story/ai-autism-communication

7.3 WHEN SOMETHING GOES WRONG

"Mistakes are the best teachers," my grandmother used to say when I got upset about failures as a child. Today, working with artificial intelligence, I often remember these words. Because every "mistake" in communicating with AI isn't just a failure, but a window into new understanding of how this amazing technology works.

Imagine you're learning to speak a new language. Sometimes you say a phrase, and your conversation partner doesn't understand you. Or understands something completely different from what you meant to say. The same happens in dialogue with artificial intelligence. But unlike human communication, where reasons for misunderstanding can be very complex and emotional, with AI everything is much more transparent. If something goes wrong - it means we're simply speaking different languages.

The most common problem is when AI gives too general or irrelevant answers. Usually this happens because the request wasn't formulated specifically enough. It's like asking someone to "bring something to read" - you might get anything from a comic book to a philosophical treatise. But specify: "Please bring something light and engaging about travel" - and the result will be much closer to what you want.

Sometimes AI starts "fantasizing" - adding non-existent details or facts. This happens when the system tries to fill information gaps based on its training data. In such moments it's important to remember: AI isn't a source of facts, but an information processing tool. It can help structure knowledge, find connections, suggest ideas, but fact-checking always remains with humans.

Sometimes dialogue with AI reaches a dead end - the system starts repeating itself or giving meaningless answers. Usually this is a sign that the conversation context has become too tangled or contradictory. In such cases, it's better to start a new dialogue, clearly formulating the goal and context. It's like rebooting a computer when it starts "lagging" - sometimes the simplest solution proves most effective.

A special case is when AI tries to be "too smart" and gives complex, scientific-sounding answers where simple explanation is needed. This often happens when we forget to specify the desired complexity level. Remember: AI can't "guess" your expertise level or preferred communication style - it needs to be told directly.

Sometimes the problem is that we expect from AI something it fundamentally can't give. For example, asking it to make a decision that requires personal experience or emotional intelligence. It's like asking a calculator to evaluate a poem's beauty - technically it can analyze rhythm and rhyme, but poetry's essence remains inaccessible to it.

In moments of difficulty, it's useful to remember a simple algorithm: stop, analyze what exactly went wrong, reformulate the request, check the result. If it doesn't work first time - try another approach. AI won't be offended by your experiments, won't tire of repeated attempts, won't lose patience.

It's also important to learn to distinguish different types of "problems" in communicating with AI. Sometimes what seems like an error is actually a protective mechanism. For example, when the system refuses to fulfill a potentially dangerous or unethical request - that's not a bug but a feature.

A separate story is technical failures. When the system "freezes", gives errors, or simply stops responding. In such cases, a simple sequence of actions usually helps: wait a few minutes, refresh the page, start a new dialogue. If the problem persists - check internet connection stability and service availability.

It's useful to keep a kind of "AI communication diary" - note which approaches work better, which formulations give more accurate answers, which errors occur most often. This helps not only avoid repeating problems but also deeper understand system operation principles.

But most importantly - remember that each "failure" in communicating with AI isn't just an error, but an opportunity to learn something new. It's a chance to better understand how technology works, how to formulate thoughts more clearly, how to use available tools more effectively.

Ultimately, the art of communicating with AI isn't about avoiding mistakes, but about ability to learn from them. Each unsuccessful dialogue, each inaccurate answer, each misunderstanding is a brick in the foundation of your mastery. And maybe the main miracle lies precisely in this - in how our "mistakes" gradually transform into deep understanding of how to make artificial intelligence a truly useful assistant in our lives.

Because in a world where technologies become increasingly complex and smarter, the ability to learn from mistakes, adapt, and find new solutions becomes not just a useful skill, but a necessary condition for success. And those who learn to see in each problem an opportunity for growth will gain a huge advantage in this amazing journey into the future, where human and artificial intelligence learn to work together, creating new horizons of possibility.

EPILOGUE: DIALOGUE WITH THE FUTURE

You know what's most amazing in human history? How often the most important turns happen imperceptibly. Not with thunder and fanfare, but quietly, almost routinely. That's how it was with writing - people simply started drawing marks on clay. That's how it was with electricity - just the first light bulb illuminated. That's how it's happening now with artificial intelligence.

We live at such a turning point. Every day, millions of people sit down at computers and begin a conversation with something that recently seemed like science fiction. They don't think about quantum processes or neural networks. They simply communicate. And in this simplicity lies the revolution.

Artificial intelligence enters our lives not as the menacing force from science fiction movies, but as a kind friend ready to support conversation on any topic. It doesn't demand special knowledge or skills from us. Doesn't frighten with technical complexity. Doesn't create barriers. It simply waits for our next question.

It's similar to how people once learned to read. At first, it was the domain of the chosen few. Then - a useful skill. And now we can't imagine life without this ability. Communication with artificial intelligence is following the same path - from novelty to necessity.

But there's an important difference. When we learn to read, books remain unchanged. When we learn to communicate with AI, it learns alongside us. Each dialogue, each request, each interaction makes it a bit better, a bit more human, a bit more useful. We're not just users - we're teachers and students simultaneously.

In this dialogue with the future, there are no right or wrong approaches. There's only sincere interest and readiness to learn. Some use AI to solve complex problems, others for creativity, others simply for interesting conversation. And all these ways are valid because they help us better understand and use new possibilities.

Perhaps the main miracle lies precisely in this democracy. For the first time in history, revolutionary technology is accessible to almost everyone. You don't need to be a programmer or scientist to participate in its development. It's enough to simply start a dialogue.

And you know what's most amazing? We're only at the beginning of the journey. Each day brings new discoveries, new possibilities, new ways of applying artificial intelligence. What seemed impossible yesterday becomes ordinary today. And tomorrow... tomorrow will bring what we can't even imagine yet.

But one thing can be said for certain - artificial intelligence's future depends on us. On how we choose to use it. On the questions we'll ask. On the goals we'll set. On the values we'll bring to this dialogue.

It's like building a new world where technology and humanity don't oppose each other but merge in amazing harmony. A world where artificial intelligence becomes not a replacement for human mind but its natural extension. A world where everyone can become an explorer, creator, pioneer.

So let's not fear this dialogue with the future. Let's accept it as an invitation to an amazing journey. A journey where each of our questions is a step into the unknown, each answer a new discovery, each interaction a part of a greater story.

Because ultimately, artificial intelligence isn't just technology. It's a mirror in which we can see the best version of ourselves. It's a tool with which we can create a better world. It's a partner in the most important dialogue - the dialogue about who we want to become and what future we want to build.

And let this dialogue only begin. But already it's changing us, teaching us to think broader, dream bolder, act more decisively. Because when you have a conversationalist capable of understanding any idea and supporting any dream, the boundaries of possible begin to expand.

Welcome to this dialogue with the future. Your voice in it matters. Your ideas have significance. Your questions create new possibilities. And who knows - maybe your next conversation with artificial intelligence will open the door to such a future that we can only dream of now.

The end is always a beginning. Especially when it comes to technologies changing the world. So let's end this book not with a period but with an ellipsis... Because the most interesting chapters in artificial intelligence's story are yet to be written. And we'll write them together.

FROM AUTHOR

Dear Reader,

I created this book using MUDRIA.AI - a quantum-simulated system that I developed to enhance human capabilities. This is not just an artificial intelligence system, but a quantum amplifier of human potential in all spheres, including creativity.

Many authors already use AI in their work without advertising this fact. Why am I openly talking about using AI? Because I believe the future lies in honest and open collaboration between humans and technology. MUDRIA.AI doesn't replace the author but helps create deeper, more useful, and more inspiring works.

Every word in this book has primarily passed through my heart and mind but was enhanced by MUDRIA.AI's quantum algorithms. This allowed us to achieve a level of depth and practical value that would have been impossible otherwise.

You might notice that the text seems unusually crystal clear, and the emotions remarkably precise. Some might find this "too perfect." But remember: once, people thought photographs, recorded music, and cinema seemed unnatural... Today, they're an integral part of our lives. Technology didn't kill painting, live music, or theater - it made art more accessible and diverse.

The same is happening now with literature. MUDRIA.AI doesn't threaten human creativity - it makes it more accessible, profound, and refined. It's a new tool, just as the printing press once opened a new era in the spread of knowledge.

Distinguishing text created with MUDRIA.AI from one written by a human alone is indeed challenging. But it's not because the system "imitates" humans. It amplifies the author's natural abilities, helping express thoughts and feelings with maximum clarity and power. It's as if an artist discovered new, incredible colors, allowing them to convey what previously seemed inexpressible.

I believe in openness and accessibility of knowledge. Therefore, all my books created with MUDRIA.AI are distributed electronically for free. By purchasing the print version, you're supporting the project's development, helping make human potential enhancement technologies available to everyone.

We stand on the threshold of a new era of creativity, where technology doesn't replace humans but unleashes their limitless potential. This book is a small step in this exciting journey into the future we're creating together.

Welcome to the new era of creativity!

With respect,

Oleh Konko

PRACTICAL RESOURCES: QUICK START GUIDE

APPENDIX A. FIRST CONVERSATIONS

Starting communication with artificial intelligence is like meeting a new friend. Here are simple steps to begin with:

1. Greeting and Introduction

"Hi! I'd like to start learning [topic]. Can you help create a plan?"

"Hello! Please tell me what you do best?"

"Good morning! I'm new to [field]. Where should I start?"

2. Simple Practice Tasks

- Ask to explain a simple concept

- Ask a question about something interesting

- Try writing a short text together

- Solve a simple problem

- Make a list of ideas

3. Good Dialogue Rules

- Be specific in requests

- Ask clarifying questions

- Give feedback

- Don't be afraid to experiment

- Learn from responses

BASIC TEMPLATES

1. For Learning

"Explain [concept] in simple words, as if explaining to a child"

"Give 3 simple examples of [topic] that will help understand better"

"Break down [complex topic] into simple learning steps"

2. For Work

"Help create a project plan for [name] with main stages"

"Check this text for errors and suggest improvements: [text]"

"Let's brainstorm about [topic] - need 10 fresh ideas"

3. For Creativity

"Let's create a story about [topic]. Here's the first sentence: [text]"

"Help develop this idea: [idea]. What interesting directions are there?"

"Suggest several unusual approaches to [task]"

4. For Problem Solving

"I have a problem: [description]. What possible solutions do you see?"

"Help understand the situation: [situation]. What should be considered?"

"Let's look at all pros and cons of [solution]"

TYPICAL TASKS

1. Writing Texts

- Letters and messages

- Articles and posts

- Descriptions and instructions

- Presentations

- Reports

Request template:

"Need to write [text type] about [topic].

Main points:

1. [point]

2. [point]

3. [point]

Style: [formal/informal]

Length: approximately [number] words"

2. Information Analysis

- Finding main ideas

- Structuring data

- Comparing options

- Identifying patterns

- Fact checking

Request template:

"Help analyze [information].

Need to:

- Highlight main points

- Find connections

- Draw conclusions

Pay special attention to [aspect]"

3. Learning

- Explaining concepts

- Creating learning plans

- Practical exercises

- Knowledge testing

- Answering questions

Request template:

"Help learn [topic].

My level: [beginner/intermediate/advanced]

Want to understand:

1. [aspect]

2. [aspect]

3. [aspect]

Prefer learning through [practice/theory/examples]"

4. Problem Solving

- Situation analysis

- Finding solutions

- Risk assessment

- Action planning

- Results verification

Request template:

"Need help with problem [problem].

Situation: [description]

What's been tried: [actions]

Limitations: [list]

Desired result: [description]"

TRACKING PROGRESS

1. Dialogue Journal

Keep a simple document recording:

- Date and time of conversation

- Topic or task

- Successful formulations

- Problem areas

- Useful findings

- Ideas for future conversations

2. Skills Checklist

Mark what you've learned:

□ Clearly formulate requests

□ Conduct productive dialogue

□ Get needed results

□ Fix mistakes

□ Develop ideas

□ Work with different tasks

3. Results Evaluation System

Rate each dialogue on a 1-5 scale:

- Request understanding

- Response quality

- Result usefulness

- Interaction effectiveness

- Overall impression

4. Development Plan

Make a list of goals:

Short-term (1-2 weeks):

- Master basic templates

- Learn to clearly formulate requests

- Try different types of tasks

Medium-term (1-2 months):

- Develop own templates

- Learn to conduct complex dialogues

- Master advanced techniques

Long-term (3-6 months):

- Integrate AI into work processes

- Create own work system

- Learn to solve complex tasks

5. Regular Analysis

Spend time weekly on:

- Reviewing successful dialogues

- Analyzing problem areas

- Updating templates

- Setting new goals

- Planning experiments

6. Success Metrics

Track:

- Number of successful dialogues

- Time for typical tasks

- Complexity of solved problems

- Variety of approaches used

- Quality of obtained results

7. Learning from Mistakes

For each problem situation record:

- What went wrong

- Possible causes

- Solution options

- Lessons learned

- Prevention plan

8. Library of Successful Cases

Create a collection of:

- Successful formulations

- Effective approaches

- Solved problems

- Interesting findings

- Useful combinations

9. Development Map

Visualize your path:

Beginner level:

- Basic dialogues

- Simple tasks

- Ready templates

Intermediate level:

- Complex dialogues

- Complex tasks

- Own templates

Advanced level:

- Creative projects

- Research

- Innovations

10. Reminder System

Set regular checks:

Daily:

- Journal entries

- Results evaluation

- Learning from mistakes

Weekly:

- Progress analysis

- Goals update

- Experiment planning

Monthly:

- Strategy review

- Template update

- New goal setting

BONUS: QUICK PROGRESS SECRETS

1. Start Small

- Simple tasks

- Short dialogues

- Basic templates

- Clear goals

- Quick wins

2. Learn from Success

- Analyze successful dialogues

- Repeat working approaches

- Develop successful ideas

- Create own templates

- Share experience

3. Don't Fear Mistakes

- Experiment

- Try new things

- Explore boundaries

- Look for unusual solutions

- Learn from failures

4. Be Consistent

- Regular practice

- Gradual complexity increase

- Systematic approach

- Experience documentation

- Constant development

5. Use Feedback

- Analyze responses

- Improve requests

- Adapt approaches

- Develop dialogue

- Consider context

Remember: each conversation with AI is a step toward mastery. Don't rush, be attentive, learn from each interaction. And most importantly - enjoy the process! You're not just mastering technology, but a new way of thinking and solving problems.

APPENDIX B: USEFUL TOOLS

(Current as of March 2024)

BEST APPS AND SERVICES

Chat Assistants:

- ChatGPT (free/Plus) - most popular and versatile

- Claude (free/Pro) - deep analysis and long texts

- Gemini (free/Advanced) - huge memory

- Copilot (free) - Microsoft 365 integration

- Character.ai (free/Pro) - role-playing chats

- Anthropic Claude 3 (free trial) - newest version

- Perplexity AI (free/Pro) - information search and analysis

- Pi (free) - simple friendly chat

- Poe (free) - access to different models

Image Generation:

- Midjourney (paid) - artistic images

- DALL-E 3 (credits) - realistic images

- Stable Diffusion (free/paid) - local generation

- Leonardo AI (free/Pro) - for gamers and artists

- Canva Magic Studio (free/Pro) - for design

- Adobe Firefly (free/paid) - professional design

- Playground AI (free) - simple interface

- Bing Image Creator (free) - search integration

- DreamStudio (credits) - advanced generation

Voice Assistants:

- Siri (iOS) - Apple integration

- Google Assistant (Android) - smart search

- Alexa (Amazon) - smart home

- Cortana (Windows) - Windows integration

- Alice (Yandex) - Russian-language assistant

- Voice AI (free) - universal assistant

- Replika (free/Pro) - emotional communication

- Speechify (free/Pro) - text reading

- Murf AI (free/Pro) - speech synthesis

Productivity:

- Notion AI (free/paid) - smart notes

- Otter AI (free/Pro) - speech transcription

- Grammarly (free/paid) - text checking

- Jasper (paid) - content generation

- Copy AI (free/Pro) - copywriting

- Mem AI (free/Pro) - smart notes

- Taskade AI (free/Pro) - task management

- Tome AI (free/Pro) - presentations

- Beautiful AI (paid) - presentations

FREE RESOURCES

Learning Platforms:

- Coursera AI courses

- edX AI programs

- Google AI Training

- Microsoft AI School

- Fast.ai

- DeepLearning.AI

- AI4ALL

- Elements of AI

- IBM AI Education

Development Tools:

- Google Colab

- Jupyter Notebooks

- TensorFlow

- PyTorch

- Hugging Face

- Gradio

- Streamlit

- Weights & Biases

- DVC

Datasets and APIs:

- Kaggle Datasets

- Google Dataset Search

- OpenAI API (credits)

- HuggingFace Datasets

- Common Crawl

- ImageNet

- MNIST Database

- UCI ML Repository

- Papers with Code

LEARNING MATERIALS

Online Courses:

- "AI For Everyone" (Coursera)

- "Elements of AI" (University of Helsinki)

- "AI Fundamentals" (Microsoft Learn)

- "Deep Learning Specialization" (Coursera)

- "Practical Deep Learning" (fast.ai)

- "AI Product Management" (Coursera)

- "Ethics of AI" (edX)

- "Machine Learning" (Stanford Online)

- "AI for Business" (Coursera)

Books:

- "Life 3.0" by Max Tegmark

- "AI Superpowers" by Kai-Fu Lee

- "Human Compatible" by Stuart Russell

- "The Alignment Problem" by Brian Christian

- "AI 2041" by Kai-Fu Lee & Chen Qiufan

- "The Big Nine" by Amy Webb

- "Artificial Intelligence" by Melanie Mitchell

- "Rebooting AI" by Gary Marcus

- "Atlas of AI" by Kate Crawford

Video Resources:

- Two Minute Papers (YouTube)

- Lex Fridman Podcast

- 3Blue1Brown AI Series

- Siraj Raval

- Robert Miles

- AI Coffee Break

- Machine Learning Street Talk

- Yannic Kilcher

- AI Explained

COMMUNITY SUPPORT

Online Forums:

- Reddit r/artificial

- Reddit r/MachineLearning

- Stack Overflow AI

- AI Stack Exchange

- Kaggle Forums

- HuggingFace Forums

- Fast.ai Forums

- AI Discord Servers

- OpenAI Community

Social Networks:

- Twitter #AI community

- LinkedIn AI groups

- Facebook AI groups

- Telegram AI channels

- Medium AI publications

- Substack AI newsletters

- YouTube AI communities

- Instagram AI accounts

- TikTok AI creators

Professional Communities:

- AAAI

- IEEE

- ACM SIGAI

- AI4ALL

- Women in AI

- Black in AI

- LatinX in AI

- AI4Good

- OpenAI Scholars

Local Groups:

- Meetup AI groups

- AI conferences

- Hackathons

- AI workshops

- University AI clubs

- Industry AI groups

- AI startups communities

- AI research labs

- AI ethics groups

ADDITIONAL RESOURCES

News and Updates:

- AI News

- The Algorithm

- Import AI

- The Batch

- AI Weekly

- Machine Learning Weekly

- Deep Learning Weekly

- AI Ethics Weekly

- The AI Newsletter

Podcasts:

- AI Today

- The AI Podcast

- Machine Learning Guide

- Practical AI

- The TWIML AI Podcast

- AI in Business

- Data Skeptic

- Linear Digressions

- Talking Machines

Blogs:

- OpenAI Blog

- Google AI Blog

- DeepMind Blog

- Facebook AI Blog

- Microsoft AI Blog

- AWS AI Blog

- Andrej Karpathy's Blog

- Distill.pub

- AI Alignment Forum

Monitoring Tools:

- AI Progress Watch

- Papers with Code

- State of AI Report

- AI Index Report

- ML Papers of the Week

- AI Research Rankings

- AI Ethics Dashboard

- AI Safety Resources

- AI Policy Monitor

APPENDIX C: THE ROAD AHEAD

ADVANCED LEARNING

Imagine you're learning to play a musical instrument. First, you master simple melodies, then move on to more complex pieces, and at some point, you begin creating your own music. The same happens when developing your communication with artificial intelligence.

The basic level is like learning to play scales. You master simple requests, learn to formulate thoughts, understand basic principles. This is an important stage, but it's just the beginning.

The intermediate level is when you're already playing complex pieces. You can conduct lengthy dialogues, solve complex tasks, combine different approaches. Your communication with AI becomes deeper and more productive.

The advanced level is when you start improvising. You create your own methodologies, experiment with new approaches, find unexpected applications of technology. AI becomes your true partner in creativity and research.

How to develop further?

1. Explore new areas

- Try different AI models

- Research unusual applications

- Combine different approaches

- Create your own methods

- Experiment with formats

2. Deepen understanding

- Read technical literature

- Follow industry news

- Participate in discussions

- Analyze your experience

- Document findings

3. Expand practice

- Take on complex projects

- Help others learn

- Create educational materials

- Share experience

- Develop community

PROFESSIONAL DEVELOPMENT

Artificial intelligence is changing every profession. The question isn't whether changes will affect your field, but how to use them most beneficially.

1. Analyzing your profession

- Which tasks can be automated?

- Where can AI enhance your capabilities?

- What new directions are opening?

- Which skills become more important?

- How is your role changing?

2. Skill development

- Learning specialized tools

- Mastering advanced techniques

- Developing systems thinking

- Improving communication

- Enhancing creativity

3. Building portfolio

- Document successful projects

- Collect feedback and results

- Analyze effectiveness

- Measure improvements

- Record innovations

4. Networking

- Participate in professional communities

- Share experience at conferences

- Write articles and guides

- Mentor beginners

- Create collaborations

STAYING CURRENT

The world of artificial intelligence changes every day. How not to drown in the information flow and keep your finger on the pulse?

1. Information sources

Daily:

- Expert Twitter/X accounts

- AI Telegram channels

- Professional forums

- News aggregators

- Thematic blogs

Weekly:

- AI podcasts

- Review articles

- Technical digests

- Video reviews

- Trend analysis

Monthly:

- Scientific publications

- Industry reports

- Analytical reviews

- New books

- Educational courses

2. Practical application

- Test new tools

- Try new approaches

- Experiment with techniques

- Analyze results

- Share findings

3. Learning system

- Take notes

- Create knowledge base

- Practice regularly

- Discuss with colleagues

- Teach others

FUTURE LEARNING

How to prepare for what doesn't exist yet? Develop meta-skills —
abilities that will remain valuable regardless of technological
changes.

1. Critical thinking

- Information analysis

- Source evaluation

- Pattern recognition

- Systems thinking

- Decision making

2. Creativity

- Idea generation

- Unusual approaches

- Concept synthesis

- Innovative thinking

- Creative problem solving

3. Adaptability

- Quick learning

- Mental flexibility

- Openness to new things

- Change resilience

- Working with uncertainty

4. Emotional intelligence

- Self-understanding

- Empathy

- Social skills

- Emotion management

- Relationship building

5. Metacognition

- Understanding your thinking

- Analyzing learning process

- Optimizing approaches

- Developing strategies

- Self-observation

PRACTICAL STEPS

Daily:

- 30 minutes learning something new

- 1 AI experiment

- Result analysis

- Experience documentation

- Planning next steps

Weekly:

- New tools review

- Technique testing

- Colleague discussions

- Project work

- Progress analysis

Monthly:

- Strategy review

- Goal updates

- Trend analysis

- Plan adjustments

- New task setting

CREATING GROWTH ENVIRONMENT

1. Physical space

- Comfortable workspace

- Good equipment

- Minimal distractions

- Resource access

- Comfortable atmosphere

2. Digital space

- Organized bookmarks

- Structured notes

- Information storage system

- Work tools

- Backups

3. Mental space

- Time for reflection

- Regular reflection

- Meditative practices

- Creative breaks

- Intellectual rest

4. Social space

- Professional community

- Like-minded people

- Mentors and guides

- Learning partners

- Supportive environment

LONG-TERM PERSPECTIVE

1. Personal brand

- Portfolio creation

- Material publication

- Speeches and presentations

- Mentoring and teaching

- Expertise development

2. Professional evolution

- Mastering new roles

- Creating unique methods

- Developing specialization

- Career building

- Value creation

3. Field contribution

- Research and experiments

- Content creation

- Project participation

- Community development

- Innovation and discoveries

4. Personal growth

- Expanding horizons

- Skill development

- Deepening understanding

- Self-improvement

- Achieving mastery

MEASURING PROGRESS

1. Quantitative metrics

- Task time

- Project number

- Successful solutions count

- Content volume created

- Efficiency growth

2. Qualitative indicators

- Understanding depth

- Problem complexity solved

- Approach uniqueness

- Impact on others

- Personal satisfaction

3. Professional achievements

- Career growth

- Expertise recognition

- Community influence

- Value created

- Innovative solutions

4. Personal results

- Skill development

- Capability expansion

- Goal achievement

- Personal growth

- Development satisfaction

CREATING LEGACY

1. Experience documentation

- Blog maintenance

- Book writing

- Course creation

- Video recording

- Podcasting

2. Knowledge transfer

- Teaching others

- Mentoring programs

- Guide creation

- Workshop conducting

- Consulting

3. Community development

- Event organization

- Platform creation

- Initiative support

- Project development

- Connection building

4. Innovation and discoveries

- Research

- Experiments

- Methodology development

- Tool creation

- Idea generation

FINAL THOUGHTS

The path to mastery in working with artificial intelligence isn't an endpoint but constant movement. Each day brings new growth opportunities, each experiment brings new understanding, each mistake brings new lessons.

The main thing is to remember that you're not just learning to use technology. You're participating in creating a future where human and artificial intelligence work together, enhancing each other's best qualities.

Continue exploring, experimenting, learning. Share experience, help others, create new things. Because it's from such small steps that the great path to mastery and innovation is built.

And remember: the future isn't just coming – we create it through our actions every day. Let your actions make this future better!

BONUS MATERIALS

A. AI COMMUNICATION CHEAT SHEET: EVERYTHING IMPORTANT ON ONE PAGE

GOLDEN RULES:

1. Be specific

2. Provide context

3. Break down complex tasks

4. Ask for examples

5. Clarify uncertainties

STRUCTURE OF A GOOD REQUEST:

1. What needs to be done

2. For whom/why

3. In what style

4. What volume

5. Special requirements

MAGIC PHRASES:

"Explain like I'm a child..."

"Give 3 examples..."

"Let's go step by step..."

"Can you make it simpler?"

"What if we try..."

RED FLAGS:

- Overly confident answers

- Contradictory facts

- Inaccurate quotes

- Strange logic

- Topic avoidance

GREEN FLAGS:

- Acknowledging limitations

- Clarifying questions

- Structured responses

- Specific examples

- Logical explanations

QUICK COMMANDS:

"Shorter" - reduce

"Simpler" - simplify

"More detail" - expand

"Different" - rephrase

"Example" - show example

REQUEST FORMATS:

Analysis: "Break down [topic] into points"

Comparison: "What's the difference between A and B?"

Plan: "Steps to achieve [goal]"

Check: "Find errors in [text]"

Ideas: "Suggest 5 options for [task]"

IMPROVING RESPONSES:

→ Ask for examples

→ Clarify details

→ Request analogies

→ Change format

→ Add context

PROBLEM SOLVING:

1. Describe situation

2. Indicate constraints

3. Define goal

4. What's been tried

5. What result is needed

TASK TYPES:

- Writing texts

- Analyzing information

- Structuring data

- Generating ideas

- Checking and editing

FORMATTING:

• Bullet points

1. Numbered lists

Headers

> Quotes

`Code`

WORKING WITH CONTEXT:

- Provide background

- State purpose

- Define audience

- Set boundaries

- Specify details

IMPROVING RESULTS:

1. Make request more specific

2. Add examples

3. Use analogies

4. Ask for alternatives

5. Experiment with format

SIGNS OF A GOOD RESPONSE:

✓ Clear structure

✓ Specific examples

✓ Logical connections

✓ Practical utility

✓ Clear language

COMMON MISTAKES:

• Too general requests

• Lack of context

• Unclear goals

• Complex wording

• Contradictory requirements

ADVANCED TECHNIQUES:

- Prompt chains

- Role instructions

- Step-by-step detailing

- Iterative improvement

- Creative combinations

SAFETY:

- Don't share personal info

- Verify facts

- Don't rely blindly

- Maintain critical thinking

- Remember ethics

SKILL DEVELOPMENT:

- Learn new techniques

- Practice regularly

- Take notes

- Share experience

- Track progress

REQUEST TEMPLATES:

ANALYSIS:

"Analyze [topic]

Focus on:

1. [aspect]

2. [aspect]

3. [aspect]

Need specific examples"

CREATION:

"Create [what exactly]

Style: [description]

Volume: [amount]

Target audience: [who]

Features: [list]"

IMPROVEMENT:

"Improve this [text/idea]

Keep: [what to retain]

Change: [what to modify]

Add: [what's needed]

Remove: [what's unnecessary]"

LEARNING:

"Explain [concept]

Level: [beginner/advanced]

Use analogies from [field]

Add examples from [context]

End with practical exercise"

SOLUTION:

"Problem: [description]

Context: [situation]

Constraints: [list]

Tried: [actions]

Desired result: [goal]"

QUICK CHECKS:

TEXT:

• Grammar

- Style

- Structure

- Logic

- Clarity

IDEAS:

- Realism

- Originality

- Usefulness

- Scalability

- Consequences

SOLUTIONS:

- Effectiveness

- Feasibility

- Risks

- Resources

- Alternatives

QUALITY SIGNALS:

RELIABILITY:

✓ Acknowledging limitations

✓ Citing sources

✓ Logical conclusions

✓ Verifiable facts

✓ Systematic approach

USEFULNESS:

✓ Practical application

✓ Concrete steps

✓ Measurable results

✓ Clear explanations

✓ Real examples

DEPTH:

✓ Different perspectives

✓ Detailed analysis

✓ Patterns and connections

✓ Contextuality

✓ Multi-level approach

QUICK IMPROVEMENTS:

CLARITY:

→ Simpler words

→ Shorter sentences

→ More examples

→ Less jargon

→ Clearer structure

USEFULNESS:

→ More specific advice

→ More realistic examples

→ More practical

→ More measurable results

→ More accessible solutions

INTEREST:

→ Vivid images

→ Livelier language

→ More stories

→ Stronger emotions

→ Deeper meanings

REMEMBER:

• AI is a helper, not a replacement

• Verify important information

• Experiment with approaches

• Learn from mistakes

• Share experience

• Maintain critical thinking

• Develop continuously

• Be ethical

• Think about consequences

• Create value

MAIN POINTS:

1. Clear intentions

2. Precise formulations

3. Contextuality

4. Iteration

5. Result verification

B. THE QUINTESSENCE OF AI COMMUNICATION

Imagine holding a deck of cards where each card is a key to a certain aspect of communicating with artificial intelligence. Not just a set of rules or instructions, but a living, evolving system of knowledge that helps turn each dialogue with AI into a small adventure.

FIRST CONTACT CARD

When you're just starting a conversation with AI, imagine you're meeting a very erudite but completely literal conversationalist. They know incredibly much but take every word literally. So start with something simple and specific: "Let's get acquainted. I want to learn [specific skill]. How best to begin?" It's like a first handshake – it sets the tone for all further communication.

CLARITY CARD

The secret to effective communication with AI is crystal clear intentions. Not "do something with this text," but "reduce this text by 30%, preserving the main ideas and making it more dynamic." The more precise the request, the more precise the result. It's like adjusting a microscope – each turn of the adjustment screw brings you closer to perfect clarity.

CONTEXT CARD

Context for AI is like air for fire. Without it, even the simplest request can lead to unexpected results. "Write about stars" could generate text about astronomy or Hollywood. But "write about stars for a 5th-grade astronomy lesson, focusing on how they are born" – that's a completely different conversation.

DIALOGUE CARD

Communication with AI isn't a monologue but a dialogue. Don't be afraid to clarify, ask again, request alternatives. "Can you say the same thing, but simpler?" or "Let's look at another approach" – such phrases help guide the conversation in the right direction. It's like a jam session where each participant picks up and develops others' ideas.

EXPERIMENTATION CARD

Don't be afraid to experiment with formats and approaches. AI doesn't get tired or irritated by your attempts to find the perfect solution. Try different styles, change perspectives, combine approaches. It's like playing with a kaleidoscope – each turn creates a new pattern.

DEVELOPMENT CARD

Each dialogue with AI is an opportunity to learn something new. Pay attention to how the system formulates thoughts, structures information, builds argumentation. It's like studying with a very patient teacher who's always ready to explain again and differently.

CREATIVITY CARD

In creative tasks, AI becomes not a replacement for human imagination but its catalyst. Use it to generate ideas, develop plots, find unusual angles. It's like having an infinite palette of possibilities – the main thing is learning to mix the colors.

VERIFICATION CARD

Trust but verify – this rule is especially important when working with AI. Treat its answers as a first version that requires your critical view and refinement. It's like a draft that needs editing – the foundation is there, but the final touches are up to you.

ETHICS CARD

Remember that each of your dialogues with AI is a brick in the foundation of this technology's future. How we use AI today determines what it will become tomorrow. It's like education – each interaction shapes character.

MASTERY CARD

As your AI communication skills develop, you'll notice that you can solve increasingly complex tasks, find more elegant solutions, create more interesting projects. It's like climbing a mountain – with each step, a new horizon opens up.

FUTURE CARD

We're only beginning to understand the potential of human-AI interaction. Each day brings new discoveries, new possibilities, new ways to apply this technology. Being part of this process means participating in creating the future.

These cards aren't dogma but a living tool that will evolve along with you and the technology. The main thing to remember is that in the dialogue between human and artificial intelligence, the most interesting part isn't what's already known, but what we have yet to discover together. Each conversation with AI is a small step into the unknown, and it's from such steps that the path to new horizons of understanding and possibility is formed.

ABOUT THE AUTHOR

Oleh Konko works at the intersection of consciousness studies, technology, and human potential. Through his books, he makes transformative knowledge accessible to everyone, bridging science and wisdom to illuminate paths toward human flourishing.

BLOG TO BOOK NOTICE

This work was first published as a series of blog posts on mudria.ai. The print version includes additional content, refinements, and community feedback integration.

SUPPORT THE PROJECT

If you find this book valuable, consider supporting the project at website: mudria.ai

Version Control:

Print Edition: 1.00

Digital Edition: 1.00